Piracy
Days of Long Ago

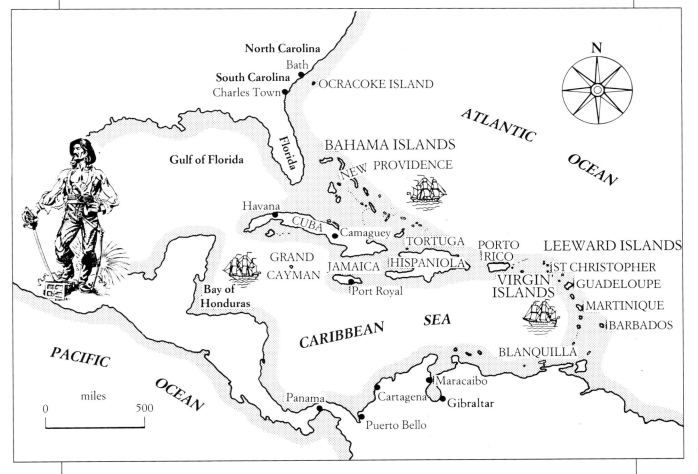

Kenneth W. Mulder
Author

Sandra Mulder
Editor

Rick Reeves
Richard Becker
Gene Packwood
Artists and Illustrators

Foreword

Many books on piracy are loaded with romanticism and mysticism, or — as the author of *Piracy — Days of Long Ago* says — retell the time-worn, hand-me-down myths which only glamorize the original characters. Such is not the mission of Kenneth W. Mulder's excellent treatment of the wide-ranging subject. His masterful and scholarly work is designed to rip away the veneer and mythical tales of the sea that have been glorified and magnified since days of yore.

This is solid history and reflects extensive research and minute detail on the role piracy played in the development and settlement of the New World and the distribution of its wealth.

The author traces the evolution of vessels from the floating log . . to one hollowed out to a canoe . . then came the raft . . to which was added a sail. Mulder peppers his volume with history of water transportation, as well as contemporary news of what was happening in the ever-expanding world even as events at sea were capturing the fascination and imagination of early civilization.

There are surprises tucked away in the script. History majors will learn fresh, new facts about Christopher Columbus, for instance. The truth behind the glamour of piracy is told revealing the hard, cruel life of the pirates presented in the context of the realities of the turbulence of their time.

The book also features fresh, authentic full-color art work for your enjoyment. For more on this remarkable era of pirates, buccaneers and other sea-going thugs, sail on and on.

HAMPTON DUNN

Past President, Florida Historical Society and Official Historian
Hillsborough County, Florida

The author, Kenneth W. Mulder, is a native of Tampa, Florida. Since his youth he has had a strong fascination with pirates. He accumulated a substantial library on the subject and after four years of research and travel, in 1995 published the first edition of *Piracy — Days of Long Ago*.

He is a past president of the Tampa Historical Society, has served as trustee of the Henry B. Plant Museum, and is a member of the Florida Historical Society, the Sun Coast Archaeological & Paleontological Society and Florida Anthropological Society. He is a past member of the Hillsborough County Historical Commission and has published many articles and booklets on early Tampa and Florida history, including *"Tampa Historical Guide"*, *"Aboriginal Artifacts of Tampa Bay"*, *"Tampa Bay — Days of Long Ago"* and *"Seminoles — Days of Long Ago"*.

Kenneth W. Mulder

His wife, Sandra, edits his publications and together, they are pleased to offer the second edition of *Piracy — Days of Long Ago* for your reading pleasure.

Welcome aboard, Mate!

Piracy
Days Of Long Ago

Pirates have operated on all the oceans and seas of the world, but there were certain areas which became notorious for piracy and we have chosen to tell the tales of the pirates of the Caribbean Sea in days of long ago.

The New World

Columbus expressed in his journal a sense of wonder upon exploring the Caribbean Sea.
"In it there are many harbors on the coast of the seas, and many rivers, good and large. Its islands are high and there are very lofty mountains. All are most beautiful, of a thousand shapes. And all are accessible and filled with trees of a thousand kinds and tall, and they seem to touch the sky. And some were flowering and some bearing fruit. The birds of a thousand kinds were singing. All are wonderful to behold on account of their beautiful variety."

Early History of
PIRACY

Piracy is as old as ancient man who pushed the first log into the water and paddled to the other side of the river. The one who decided to steal his neighboring tribe's food, weapons and anything else appealing to his fancy and then paddled back to his camp. Life among the human as well as the animal kingdom has always been "survival of the fittest," and in some cases, the fittest was the bully or the thief or the burglar on land, and the pirate on the sea.

Footprints of Man

Undisputed anthropological evidence of a trail of footprints of three people was found in 1978 in a layer of gray volcanic ash in the Laetoli fossil beds in northern Tanzania by paleontologist Dr. Mary D. Leakey, widow of her lifetime partner, Dr. Louis S. B. Leakey. These footprints were left by people who walked across the damp ash with an upright free stride some 3.5 million years ago. These are the earliest human footprints known to the world and clearly show the raised arch, round heel, forward-pointing big toes, and a strong heel-to-toe strike. From these individuals are the descendants who invented the boat from a floating log, later hollowed it out for a canoe, then built a raft, then added a sail.

God gave man dominion over all the creatures of the world and a brain and the ability to reason and choose. Man wandered away from his documented birth place in central Africa in small clans. The use of animal hides for clothes, animal stomach skins to hold water, and the knowledge of how to make fire had been discovered in an earlier time.

Man's tenacity of purpose, power of reasoning granted by our Creator, and his vision and imagination continued to increase in the face of difficulty and disaster, enabling him to survive the four great ice ages which covered great areas of the northern hemisphere.

When early man began to make weapons of stone-flints, his ability to kill the animals greatly increased and as his numbers grew, the need to seek new hunting areas became urgent. His only mode of travel was walking and running — the same as the animals he pursued in their foraging migration.

Early Water Transportation

Banding together in family tribes and following the animals toward the morning sun, early man happened upon a large river. The tribe had walked across small streams and ventured around lakes, but the swift flowing river halted them. They squatted down at the bank and gazed across at the animals grazing on the opposite shore. They were ready to pursue them with their spears and knives tipped with flint points, but the animals were safely out of reach.

They watched jealously as the water birds glided along the water's surface. A fallen log came floating by and on the log was a family of chattering monkeys. As the log drifted close to the opposite bank, the monkeys jumped off and scampered into the trees, hardly noticed by the grazing animals nearby which the hunters sought for food. The entire group watched, then their leader stood as the power of reasoning had begun. He looked around and found a large fallen tree trunk on his side of the river. Working together as a group they slid the tree into the water. Bravely they dared imitate the monkeys by entrusting themselves to this mysterious apparatus.

Some held onto its branches and some rode on the top side like the monkeys, and using their hands, they powered the tree log to the opposite shore and got off, pulling their log to the shore for the return trip. Others of the group found a tree log and floated over. Around their campfire that night, they discussed their new mode of travel, the floating tree, and imagined all the ways they could continue to improve on it. For the first time, man could travel without personal movement, without fatigue and out of the reach of dangers on land.

Over time, they hollowed or burned out the middle of a large tree trunk to make a place to sit, finding even larger trees to make even larger floats, not only to cross the river, but to drift down it. Paddles of wood replaced the effort to move forward by hand, and poles were used to push from the bottom of a shallow river or lake. They next tied several logs together to make rafts. They added animal

Early boat building

skin on an upright stick to catch the wind and help power and maneuver the raft. Man could now walk, run and travel on water in search of food to survive. His life was vastly improved and he ventured further east out of middle Africa toward the rising sun until he crossed the Nile River and the Red Sea into the middle east.

There were thousands of tree logs used as boats and abandoned until roving tribes finally decided to settle into villages along the rivers. Building log floats was vastly improved. They were used over and over as the villages grew in size and soon splintered apart and became neighboring tribes. Boat building occupied much of their time and boat travel spread throughout known waterways.

Herein lies a story of ships and how they were used; their captains and crews and their place in a social and economic order.

Early Ships

Since man first discovered travel by water, he had advanced not only the type of conveyance used but also his daring in exploring ever greater distances. First, all known rivers, then into the bays and inlets of the gulfs. With even stronger, larger and more reliable vessels, he had ventured into the open water of the seas off the coasts of Africa and Europe. Ever larger ships were built and man traveled a great distance to acquire costly cargo for trade.

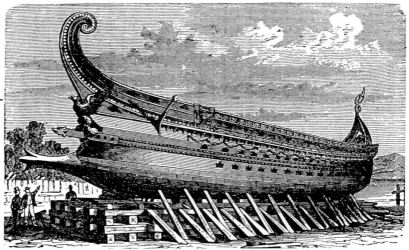
Ancient Roman ship

Where wealth existed, sea merchants risked the strength of their ship, the weather, and their own navigational skills to secure desirable cargo.

Given man's nature, it was only natural that some would find stealing the cargo easier than making the trip himself — so piracy, or theft on the sea, was the plague of the merchant seaman from the beginning.

Piracy was known in all parts of the early known world. Historical records show that it has existed wherever the rewards of crime have been worth the risk of punishment. Organized piracy was wide spread among the early settlements of humans in the Middle East and was accepted by sea merchants and slavers as an occupational hazard.

In Sumer, where cuneiform writing was first developed about five thousand years ago, was a loosely knit group of cities located along and between the Tigris and Euphrates rivers in Asia Minor. The area is today encompassed and occupied by Iraq. From Baghdad to the Persian Gulf, the land was Sumerian. Fragile fragments of cuneiform clay tablets tell of the trade and travel by sea of the

Code of Hammurabi

barbaric tribes of sea people called "Guti" who could not be held back over five thousand

years ago. They invaded on land and sea in Sumer and caused misery, destruction, famine and death. These clay tablets are the first written history of piracy, with later written records appearing with the Babylonians and Egyptians.

The first written law against piracy was included in the Code of Laws of Hammurabi, King of Babylon for about fifty years until mid-1700 B.C. His Code was engraved in cuneiform on a black diorite (stone) stele which can be viewed in the Louvre Museum in Paris — a most impressive historical legal document.

In the last century of the Roman Empire, the pirates in the Mediterranean Sea were able to plunder over five hundred villages of the Roman Empire. They even captured and held Julius Caesar for six weeks and collected a ransom.

Navigational Aids

Through the ages, scientists and astronomers discovered new aids to navigation. Others refined and improved them, granting seamen more accurate and reliable means of travel by sea. These navigational aids were used by the pirates too.

Early Charts and Maps

The oldest map made by man is believed to be a clay tablet

engraved over 4,500 years ago in Babylonia. The first known written detailed charts were also made by the Babylonians around 2500 B.C. The Phoenicians used sea maps or charts beginning 1200 B.C. and for a thousand years were the world's greatest sailors and trade merchants traveling from port to port. They were masters of celestial navigation using the observance of the Little Dipper and Big Dipper to sail by night. Information and hand drawn charts were exchanged between themselves. Prior to the discovery of the earliest compass, astronomers had mapped the skies, and both land and sea navigators used the stars to guide them in their travels.

The Compass

The hills of Magnesia in Asia Minor is the birthplace of the lodestone, the source of power for

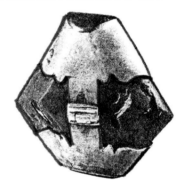

**Brassbound Lodestone
17th Century**

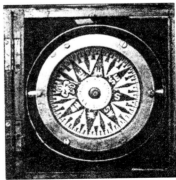

the compass. Lodestone and its magnetic properties was known to the Greeks in the seventh century B.C. and may have been known by the Chinese even earlier.

Seamen of the eleventh century were the first known to use a compass in navigation. It was simply a needle which had been rubbed against lodestone to magnatize it, thrust through a straw floating in a bowl of water. Later, the needle was pushed through a small square wooden block placed in a bowl of water, with a card placed on top of the block to show east and west. The straw caused the needle to swim and the point to turn directly toward the polar star. In the twelfth century, history reveals Arabian navigators in Chinese waters were using the same compass. Only north and south were indicated.

In 1187 English monk Alexander Neckam wrote, "Mariner's at sea, when through cloudy weather in the day, which hides the sun, or through the darkness of the night they lose knowledge of the quarter of the world to which they are sailing, touch a needle with a magnet which will turn around until, on its own motion ceasing, its point will be directed toward the north."

The north arrow was indicated by the French fleur-de-lis, chosen by the fourteenth century navigator Florio Geoga to honor the king of Naples who was of French descent.

This simple invention, the use of the natural lodestone applied to a steel needle, opened up the known nautical world to the early sailing ships. The mystery of the compass was so great that people were in awe of its power and many superstitions arose. One was if garlic or onion was rubbed on it, it would lose its power, so many seamen were forbidden to eat onion and garlic. The properties of the lodestone were said to cure dropsy, toothache, gout and convulsions.

The first reference to the use of a compass on a British sailing ship was on the *George* in 1345. For over two hundred years merchant marines complained of the poorly made device. Scientists and engineers studied the com-

pass and gradually it was improved. Its proponents of magic and mysterious power prevailed until, in 1745, Dr. Gowin Knight demonstrated to the British Royal Society how it could be improved. Using the lodestone and a large pair of magnets, the potent power was transferred to the steel needle when exposed to the lodestone. The British Royal Navy quickly endorsed it and placed new compasses with high grade steel needles on board all their ships.

The early compass was unreliable and little understood. Since its discovery many centuries before Christ, it was studied, refined, and used without confidence by early land and sea travelers. Advancement continued in the development of the compass, but even on Columbus' voyages, it was not very reliable. Weak needles lost their magnetism; sometimes one side of the needle was stronger than the other, and it was several centuries before scientists realized the needle's magnetism could be affected by lightning or nearby metal. Even in the late 1800's, pistols were still kept near the compass drawer causing navigational errors.

Other Inventions

The **astrolabe**, a graduated vertical circle with a movable arm, used to determine the altitude of the sun and stars for navigational purposes, was first used in the second century B.C. by the Greeks.

The Normans invented the ship's **rudder** in the twelfth century, locating it in the middle of the stern of a sailing vessel, thus doing away with the side steering oar. This revolutionized the steerage of a ship.

In 1608 Dutchman Hans Lippershey perfected the **telescope** and advanced naval warfare a thousand years. It was also referred to as the long glass

or spy glass, particularly when used by the pirates to spy on their prey from some distance.

In 1643 Italian Evangelista Torricelli perfected the **barometer** which measures changes in air pressure, an aid to weather forecasting.

In 1731 John Hadley of England perfected the **sextant**, an instrument which measures the separation of two distant objects, and helps determine the time of day and geographical latitude.

In 1735 England's John Harrison perfected the **chronometer**, an instrument which registers time intervals and measures longitude. He won first prize of £20,000 in a contest held by the British admiralty. The contest was the result of a great tragedy near the Scilly Islands off England when four British ships miscalculated their longitude and all went aground, killing two thousand seamen.

In the eighteenth century, the ship's **wheel** which activated pulleys to move the rudder replaced the clumsy deck-wide sweep of the old-fashioned tiller.

In 1805 Sir Frances Beaufort of England devised the **Beaufort scale**, a device to measure velocity of wind with a scale of zero to twelve; zero equals calm and twelve equals hurricane strength.

Advcancement in Sea Travel

Since man first ventured onto the water on a log, sea travel advanced more rapidly in some ways than even travel on land. On the sea, one could certainly travel a long distance faster and more directly, but not necessarily more comfortably or safer. The design and construction of ships has always been big business and the development and training of good seamen has been ongoing throughout history.

PIRATES

in the New World

In the sixth century B.C., Greek mathematician Pythagoras stated the earth was round. Aristotle, in the third century B.C., taught his pupils there were land masses west of Europe. In the first century A.D., Roman historian Pliny the Elder wrote, "the oceans surround the world earth." Educated men wrote about it; they knew it was theoretically possible to sail west from Europe to a land which it was known could be reached by land to the east, but no one considered it practical with such means as were then available — except the Italian from Genoa, Cristoforo Colombo, Cristóbal Colón to the Spaniards, and Christopher Columbus to us.

WOODCUT BY TOBIAS STIMMER
LIBRARY OF CONGRESS

The Far East is Also The Far West

Columbus was an extraordinarily versatile man. Having gone to sea at an early age, he was a knowledgeable and experienced seaman as well as chart maker. He reached the age of twenty-five totally illiterate as did the vast majority of the population of his day, and then set about learning to speak, read and write in three languages: Portuguese (the language of navigation), Castilian Spanish (the parlance of the upper class in Spain and Portugal), and Latin (the language of scholars).

Not a wealthy man, Columbus traveled for seven years to Italy, France, Portugal, and Spain seeking a government to sponsor his goal of sailing west to reach the East Indies. All listened and then dismissed his ideas time after time; rejection and dismay were his constant companions. The learned did not disagree with his theory, only that the distance was beyond reach!

Queen Isabella of Castile (Spain) was sympathetic and listened with womanly intuition. She shared with him an oddity (for a Latin person) of

reddish hair and light freckles. Twice this determined Genoese sea captain appeared before her concerning his plan to cross the Atlantic Ocean. "After all," she thought, "this Genoese may be right." His reputation as a skilled navigator was established and he offered evidence of green branches which had floated up on the coast of Africa coming on the ocean currents from the west. The ships and supplies he asked for were inexpensive, the honors he requested if successful were not unreasonable, and the glory and resources for Spain could be substantial. If he failed, very little would be lost.

Queen Isabella finally agreed to finance the voyage and to do so, the butcher shops of Seville were taxed on meat sold to pay the wages of the crews of Columbus' three ships.

The monarchs decreed that his voyage would be for the glory of Spain and the Roman Catholic Church. They agreed to grant Columbus titles of admiral, governor, and viceroy over all the lands he might explore and acquire, plus a percentage of the profits forever. They gave him a prestigious letter of introduction directed to the monarchs of Japan and China, affixed with their seals and lettered in gold on a colored scroll, declaring his an official voyage for Spain to regions of India for the purpose of trading for highly desired spices.

The First Voyages to the New World

On August 3, 1492, at age forty-one, Columbus sailed south from Palos (Spain) as commander of his flagship, the *Santa María*, a three-masted, square-rigged, decked carrack of about eighty tons with a crew of fifty; and two caravels, the *Pinta*, lateen-rigged with a crew of thirty under Martín Alonza Pinzón; and the *Niña*, square-rigged, forty ton, with twenty-four men, under Martin's brother Vicente Yáñez Pinzón. They anchored at the Canary Islands to replenish their supplies and water, reassure the crews, and re-rig the *Pinta* with a square sail as it was found to be more suitable for running before the trade winds.

They sailed due west from the Canary Islands because according to the best available charts, these islands were the same latitude as Japan and China which he would reach prior to his goal of India. Their course lay along the northern edge of the band of northeast trade winds which blew steadily in the late summer from the west coast of Africa west across the Atlantic.

After many days of sailing, the Spaniards were relieved that they had not encountered the "green sea of darkness," a name given by the Arabs for the Atlantic Ocean who believed the ocean to be terrifying, destructive, rimmed in

The Sea of Darkness

fire, and a place of no return. The sun rose and set each day with normality although the crew was watchful the entire voyage, expecting the worst.

On the afternoon of October 12, a flock of colorful parrots were seen flying southwest as if seeking a place to roost for the night. One of the Pinzón brothers persuaded the Admiral to change his course and follow the parrots. Had Columbus not changed course slightly, the landfall would have been in Florida or the Carolinas because he would have sailed into the Gulf Stream which flows northward four miles an hour. That one flock of tropical parrots determined the distribution of the New World — the Latin countries settling in Central and South America, and the English, Dutch, Germans, and French in North America.

There was a full moon on the night of October 12 and the high cliffs shone brightly in its light on the island of the Bahamas that Columbus named *San Salvador*, or Holy Saviour, in gratitude for safely sailing west for seventy-one days from Europe. A royal annuity of ten thousand maravedis was to be granted to the first to sight land and this honor went to Juan Rodriquez Bermeo, a sailor aboard the *Pinta*. Bermeo never received the money; Columbus claimed it for himself.

The New World Beckons

Upon landing at San Salvador, Columbus, the Pinzón brothers and some of the crew met the gentle Taino people who spoke excitedly in an unknown tongue and were as completely naked as when their mothers bore them. Columbus called these people *los Indios*, or Indians, thinking he had landed in the Indian Ocean. He and his men were welcomed with food, gifts and friendship. Sadly, within forty years the entire Taino population would be dead from new diseases unintentionally introduced by the early explorers.

After exploring San Salvador for several weeks, Columbus claimed San Salvador for the sovereigns of Spain. He persuaded several of the natives to guide him south through the maze of other unknown islands. They piloted him to Cuba's northwestern coast where he landed. The villages of palmetto-thatched huts they found bore little likeness to the *cambaluk* Marco Polo described where he

met the Great Khan. The natives did not have slanted eyes! And the Emperor of China was not to be found!

On the return trip to the ships, the envoys observed the natives of Cuba who lit one end of a tightly rolled brown leaf and inhaled the smoke through their nostrils. They were  introduced to an ecstacy and delight explained as tobacco. An entry in Columbus' journal noted the natives slept in woven grass mats hung from trees (this led to the adoption of the hammock as a standard bed for seamen).

Leaving the coast of Cuba, the Taino natives guided Columbus across the Windward Passage to the island we today call Hispaniola, with Haiti on its western end and Dominican Republic on the east. Columbus named it *La Isla Española*, or The Spanish Island. There he explored and found grains of gold in rivers coming down from the jungle mountains of the interior, and the native Arawaks wore gold jewelry on their arms and legs and in their nose and ears. The excitement of the discovery of

gold on the island of Hispaniola made the crew careless. While sailing along the coast on Christmas Eve 1492, a young cabin boy was left at the tiller without supervision. He ran the *Santa María* onto a large coral reef. On a falling tide, the ship soon broke apart.

Columbus took this as a religious omen that he should take the ship's timbers and build a colony, *La Villa de Navidad*, or Village of the Nativity. He left thirty-nine men in this new colony, vowed to return, and left for Spain to report on things he had witnessed in the New World. He took with him gold, parrots, tobacco, exotic tropical fruits and Arawak men, women and children "Indians" in chains to prove his claims of reaching the Indies.

Transferring the flag of Admiral to the *Niña*, Columbus sailed with the *Pinta* north to the latitude nearest the island of Bermuda, turning east across the Atlantic on the westerly winds of winter through two very bad storms. During the first storm, lots were drawn from a leather cup filled with peas; one had a tiny cross, and the person drawing this pea promised to walk barefoot to the first Shrine of the Virgin they reached to give thanks for safe passage. Columbus drew the marked pea.

The Santa María

Returning to the Old World

The Portuguese Azores allowed Columbus and his men to land and fulfill their vow for the visit to the shrine. Later some were arrested and placed in jail, the Portuguese being suspicious that they were Spanish smugglers or pirates. Loose talk among the sailors about the gold of the New World gave the jailers many rumors which spread quickly among the other islands of the Azores. The real pirates in port listened intently to stories about the New World and plans were made for the future and their dastardly deeds. Columbus freed his men from jail and set sail north for Palos. Encountering more storms, the *Niña* sailed into the port of Restello, four miles from Lisbon, on March 4, 1493, with one remaining tattered sail, all others torn to shreds, its crew a dreadful lot to behold.

The Portuguese in Lisbon were impressed with the successes of Columbus' voyage to the New World, but envious. The *Niña* was refitted with new sails, the rigging repaired, and they sailed for Palos where Columbus and his men were received as heroes on March 15, 1493. He received payment for this voyage of 2,000 Spanish maravedis or approximately $59 in today's money for exploring the New World.

Many refer to Columbus' explorations as "discoveries," but Columbus did not discover a new world; he established contact between two worlds, both already old. Sadly, the Spaniards had no reluctance to claim and inhabit these lands since the natives were considered by the Catholic Church to be heathens without a soul, and the native's land (which they considered sacred) was violated.

Two recent inventions spread this news quickly throughout Europe — the printing press and wax candles used to see at night and to read by (for the few other than church officials who could read). Artists' drawings and stories of Columbus' explorations and conquests were reproduced in every language in Europe. Three more voyages lay ahead, but his fame had already reached its zenith and beyond lay humiliation and defeat.

The anxious pirates and spies were in the crowd watching. They, too, would soon sail to the New world in stolen fast sleek ships, with powerful cannons and vengeful bloodthirsty crews seeking adventure and loot. And Spain was going to supply it for the next three hundred years.

Just before the

beginning of Columbus' second voyage, Spain quickly petitioned the Pope in Rome to confer on Spain the total sovereignty of all the new lands explored and claimed by Columbus, lands 100 leagues west of the Cape Verde Islands off Africa's west coast. Their rival, Catholic Portugal, violently protested to the Pope and in 1494, the line was moved by mutual consent with Spain to 270 leagues further west. This gave Portugal all of the territory of Brazil.

The Second Voyage, 1493 - 1496

At the command of the sovereigns, the Admiral quickly prepared to return to the New World by outfitting seventeen sturdy ships, including the faithful *Niña*, loaded with would-be settlers and all manner of supplies — fruit trees, seeds and cuttings of plants, shoots of sugar cane from the Canary Islands, chickens, ducks, goats, cattle, oxen, horses, sheep, mules and hogs, along with twelve hundred men and Roman Catholic priests to convert the Indians.

Volunteers from all walks of life joined — soldiers, physicians, artisans, miners, farmers; strong men of vision and adventure. Excitement was at its peak. Also included were some French, English, Portuguese and Dutch spies who slipped aboard as crew members, their mission sponsored by future privateers and pirates who would soon follow.

As the ships approached south

Reception by Sovereigns

of the latitude of Hispaniola, Columbus sighted and named the island of Dominica. The monks sailing with him had requested an island named for their holy shrine, so he named the next island Guadeloupe. Exploring crewmen discovered that island populated by wild Caribs and evidence of cannibalism there. The next island he sighted, he christened Santa Cruz (today's St. Croix).

He sailed on to La Navidad and after firing the cannon as an approach signal and receiving no reply, he landed with a few men and discovered the village completely deserted. All of those left behind in the small settlement had been killed and the buildings burned. Some of the friendly Arawaks returned and told Columbus that his men got tired of trading for gold and began to attack neighboring tribes where they raped the women, tortured, mutilated, and committed outright murder to obtain gold more quickly.

On a dark moonless night, goaded by revenge and encouraged by their shaman, the gates of hell opened. The violent and fierce tribes had struck quickly, killing all and burning the village. Columbus was furious and ashamed of his own men he had left behind, as the first Spanish colony in the New World had become nothing more than a gold hunt.

The Admiral then sailed along the coast of Hispaniola and started a new colony east of Navidad which he named La Isabela to honor the queen. Here he unloaded all the supplies, settlers and livestock. He purchased two caravals for himself for further exploration of the route to India and then sent fifteen ships home to Spain.

Columbus sailed west of Hispaniola toward Cuba's southeastern coast. His Arawak guides took him south to view a new large island the natives called Jamaica, and on his return trip,

they sailed east toward the Lesser Antilles, sighting and naming all large islands. The beauty of the islands cast a spell over the Europeans, the lush tropical land and coasts contrasted with their harsh cold homelands. He claimed Jamaica, the Virgins and the Lesser Antilles for Spain.

Columbus returned after five months to the new colony of Isabela with very little gold. There he found the grass-roofed houses, the plaza, the church, and the crude fortress Columbus had instructed the settlers to build were in hopeless disarray.

The natives had broken into open revolt as European disease had struck many. Insects were rampant; food was running out. The new settlers were not inclined to build towns or farm; they wanted gold and went out to get it. Acts of cruelty by the Spaniards were commonplace as they had themselves become the first dreaded pirates in the New World.

In 1496 before the return to Spain from the second voyage, the Admiral appointed his brother Bartholomew governor of Isabela, which he named the capital of the New World. Columbus ordered him to move the settlement to the southern coast of Hispaniola. Bartholomew moved completely south across the island to Nueva Isabela in 1498, then in 1502, the city was moved across the Haina

River. That capital city was called Santo Domingo, where it still stands today nearly five hundred years later as the oldest city in the New World.

The Admiral spent two years in Spain conversing with the monarchs and a newly-formed Council of the Indies to deal with the new settlements and the new native converts.

By then, the Portuguese had also ventured into the New World; their able captains and navigators sailed many ships searching for new land in their conquest. They also started colonies and they, too, committed acts of piracy, stealing gold from the natives along the eastern shore of South America.

Columbus had no problem finding volunteers in Spain to go to the West Indies on the second voyage in 1493, but five years later, nobody wanted to go. The New World seemed a fraud, a delusion. "Even the gold," it was rumored, "was not good. Columbus' brothers were merciless taskmasters; neither of them were administrators and they were Italians, foreigners." The monarchs would have liked to suppress the whole affair, but the honor of Spain was at stake. After a full year of lobbying the court, Columbus obtained consent for a third voyage to find the Asiatic continents of India, China and Japan to trade for the valuable spices.

The Third Voyage, 1498 - 1500

Columbus outfitted three ships with vital supplies for Hispaniola and more settlers, many of them taken from Spain's jails to seek their destinies in the New World; for convicts, this opportunity was certainly better than prison. Three other ships took a more southerly route hoping to beat the now-active Portuguese explorers to a huge land mass that many early chartmakers believed lay across the course of the equator.

On Trinidad, only naked natives were found as on other islands, but Columbus offered to trade polished copper vessels and trinkets that made noise and glistened for their gold. The natives were unimpressed. He tried yet another idea, ordering a drummer to play and the ship's boys to dance a jig. This proved fatal; the natives responded with deadly arrows. They had heard of the brutal cruel Spaniards, and drove them away.

Looking west along a mountainous shoreline, they found the coast of present-day Venezuela on the large southern continent to be later named South America. Columbus wrote in his journal, "I am of the belief that this is a great continent of which nothing has been known until this day." After exploring for five months, Columbus set sail northward six hundred miles across open ocean to his outpost on Hispaniola to inspect the project. Complete chaos was again rampant in Santo Domingo; he found the Spanish opportunists in discontent and rebellion. The colonists' expectation of riches to be easily gathered from the ground, or better yet from the natives by barbaric torture and death, had crumbled.

On his return from the second voyage, Columbus had urgently requested the monarchs to send a courtier to the new capital as a competent administrator. Fran-cisco de Bobadilla sailed in their name to investigate the charges made against Columbus' brothers. He arrived to find seven Spanish rebels hanging from the gallows with five more to be hung the next day. Fellow Spaniards were not supposed to be hung; it was just not done. Bobadilla immediately arrested the Admiral and his brothers, Bartholomew and Diego, placing them in chains and ship-ping them home to Spain. Bobadilla released the other five rebel Spaniards and dismissed all charges against them.

On the shameful voyage to Spain, the ship's captain offered to remove the chains from the Admiral, but the Admiral refused. Inasmuch as their majesties had ordered him placed in irons, he insisted the chains remain until they were ordered removed. The Admiral so cherished those iron chains that in later years he asked that they be buried with him in his casket.

Some of the homeward-bound crew were trained spies, delighted with the opportunity to return and report to England, Holland and France of the vastness of the New World and the chaos of the Spaniard's administration of the lands they claimed. The voyage home to Spain gave Columbus ample time to nurse his bitterness, which time did not heal. Still wearing the manacles upon land-ing, he went to the hospitable monastery of Las Cuevas, across the river from Seville, to meditate his serious plight and salve his wounded ego.

For six months, the Admiral languished like a prisoner in the monastery of Las Cuevas. Finally, a royal order came that he and his brothers be released and given two thousand ducats from the crown to compensate for their impover-ished state. The famous Admiral and his brothers were ordered to appear at the Alhambra of Granada on December 17, 1500. The sound of silence was thick in the air of the throne room; the monarchs were embarrassed but very coy as the crown restored all rights and privileges to the Admi-ral and his brothers, except the governorship of Hispaniola.

The Fourth Voyage, 1502 - 1504

Columbus was over fifty years old by now with white hair, an old man by the standard of his times. Weary from the stress of redeem-ing himself and anxious to find the strait through the maze of islands he had explored and claimed for Spain, he continued to appeal to the monarchs. They began to tire of him, but his constant pleas, letters and complaints paid off. "Maybe this time he will succeed and will prove he was a worthwhile invest-ment after all," they thought. The monarchs reluctantly gave him four ships in which to find the Orient on his fourth and last voyage.

Columbus had bottled himself up in the beautiful Caribbean Sea, exploring vast amounts of land and small islands, sailing nearly in a circle seeking a route to India. This one was to be the *El Alto Viaje*, the High Voyage of Colum-bus' life and his last. The mon-archs had restricted him from landing at Santo Domingo when he arrived in the Caribbean Sea to avoid conflict with the newly-appointed governor Don Nicolás de Ovando.

He sailed offshore of the

village he had established with its expanding assemblage of wood and thatch buildings to regroup his plans and he recognized the stormy weather approaching. His joints ached, fish were close to the surface, he observed ominous swells, the western sky aflame at sunset, higher than normal tides — Columbus knew all the signs of a hurricane brewing. Word came to him that Ovando was about to send thirty ships back to Spain loaded with treasure pirated from the peaceful Arawaks. Included was Columbus' share from the island's wealth. The Spanish pirates had done well.

Columbus sent one of his captains to warn Ovando of the approaching hurricane and advise him not to let the ships sail. Ovando made light of Columbus' warning and sarcastically read Columbus' message to his audience. "What makes the foolish old Italian Admiral think he can now predict the weather for the Almighty?" said Ovando, and brazenly sent the ships on their way. Two days out, off the east coast of Florida in the Bahama Channel, the mighty hurricane struck. Twenty-five ships went down with all men and cargo lost; four more were put out of commission. Only one ship made the entire voyage to Spain and it was the one carrying the Admiral's share of pirated treasure. Now Columbus was also accused of witchcraft for saving his own gold and treasures.

The storm passed with no damage to Columbus' four ships which had headed west past the coasts of Jamaica and Cuba searching for the passage to India and the Spice Islands. They explored the Yucatan Peninsula and the coast of Central America where he found the Mayan people. In late July, they reached Roatan, an island off the coast of Honduras.

They sailed south along the coast to the Isthmus of Darien.

Only fifty miles west lay Panama and the vast Pacific Ocean, but fate would give this conquest to another explorer, Vasco Núñez de Balboa ten years later. Sailing northwest along the coast, Columbus traded for more gold with the Guaymis natives near the mouth of the Río Belén River, but the trading soon ended as the situation turned to open hostility. The natives fought ferociously and won.

Only three ships could be saved; one sank in the river. It had been over a year since the ships had been careened. The crew had to man the pumps day and night from the damage of the lowly teredo worms. Soon another ship became so worm-eaten, it too was abandoned. The two remaining ships struggled onward until the crew demanded he turn northward to Jamaica's New Seville (St. Ann's Bay) which Columbus had claimed for Spain nine years earlier. The worm-riddled caravals were run ashore on a high tide and shelters of palm fronds were constructed over the decks. Columbus suffered from arthritis, malaria, fatigue and heartbreak, and he knew his High Voyage was over.

It was April 1503; the voyage was over a year old and he would spend another year stranded at Jamaica. His son Ferdinand noted in his journal, this was "the most miserable year of my father's life," brought on by mutiny and threat of attack by Arawak natives who by now hated the Spaniards and all that they represented. Columbus threatened the natives saying he would cover the moon unless they furnished supplies (the Admiral confidently showed his "power" because reading in his almanac, he knew the exact date of an upcoming lunar eclipse as February 29, 1504). The frightened natives brought them supplies following the eclipse.

Columbus and his crew knew that to be rescued would be a miracle. They all accepted that fact except the ship's officer, Diego Méndez, who traded some armor and his brass helmet for a native canoe which he rigged with a sail and keel, and set sail with one companion on the four-hundred mile journey east to Santo Domingo. He made it there — an act of extreme skill and bravery!

Méndez rented a little caravel in Santo Domingo; a rotting hulk with tattered sails, and the bottom badly eaten by worms, with sea moss and barnacles growing below the water line so thickly she could hardly sail. But with a small crew, they sailed toward Jamaica. He rescued the Admiral and his men and returned to Hispaniola. Governor Ovando hardly gave the tired old Admiral the time of day or asked about his latest exploits. Columbus was totally rejected and ostracized; a heavy blow to so great a man.

Columbus Remembered

The Admiral sailed home to Spain for the last time in a rented ship. He was well-off financially, but this meant little. He wanted his titles, his accomplishments acknowledged, and an open apology from the crown (which never came). Instead, he watched others make new conquests and claim new lands. His friend from Genoa, Giovanni Caboto (John Cabot) had sailed in the name of English sovereigns and claimed Newfoundland and the great continent of North America for England. His old shipmate Vicente Yáñez Pinzón had sailed to Brazil in 1500 and claimed it for Portugal.

At least he was spared the knowledge that the New World he had explored was given the name of his countryman Amerigo Vespucci — not his own — by an early mapmaker!

At his death, only his sons, Diego and Ferdinand, his brother Diego and two loyal shipmates

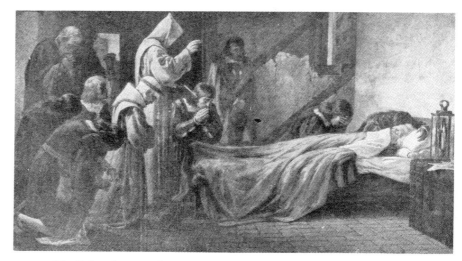

were with Columbus. The crown sent no one. On May 20, 1506, he died of sorrow, scorn and heartbreak. His last words recorded by his son were the words spoken by Christ on the cross: "Into Thy hands, Oh Lord, I commend my spirit."

Who was Christopher Columbus? A man beyond his time; a commoner who climbed to nobility. He despised those in power, but was forced to seek their help.

Deeply religious, he believed God would guide him in his sea quests to victory and felt he was empowered by the Holy Spirit. So, a man died who had totally and forever changed the course of human affairs.

Ten years after his death, historian Peter Martyr casually wrote that Admiral Don Cristóbal Colón had "departed this life". These few words were his only obituary.

The Great Explorations

With Columbus' voyages, many of the islands in the West Indies had been sighted, named, explored and claimed in the name of Spain. Spaniards had taken from the native Amerindians their most valued possession, the land itself, as though the natives had no right of legitimate ownership. But what right did the Spaniards have to move the natives over and presume to possess their lands?

Within a few years, other Spanish and Portuguese explorers came, with a wealth of treasures taken back to Europe — gold, silver, precious stones — taken from their original owners, the natives of those islands. Only items of little value to the Spaniards and usually worthless to the natives were used in trade, with the natives having no knowledge of the value of

any of their own treasures. When the natives were not willing to trade, the Spaniards took what they wanted with vengeance.

This was the age when Spain and Portugal, by rights of exploration of the New World, sailed home with bulging cargos. The time when other nations discovering the wealth

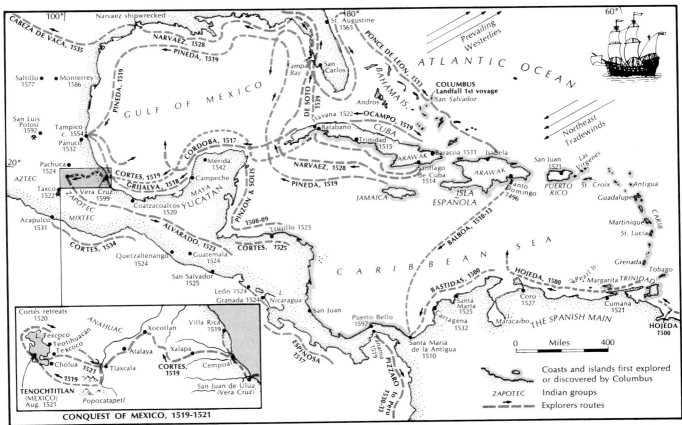

Exploration and Conquest of the New World

returning from the New World with the explorers, began to formulate plans for intercepting the returning ships to take the treasures from the Spaniards and to explore, colonize and plunder on their own. The time when Spanish ships were attacked and destroyed by pirates, the crews murdered or enslaved, and the treasures stolen. Who is to say which was the real crime?

Only a few years after Columbus' first voyage, the mysteries and treasures of the New World drew Spanish *conquistadors* or conquerors. The years 1499 through 1502 found Vicente Yáñez Pinzón, Bastidas and Alonso de Hojeda exploring the southern coasts of the Caribbean from Venezuela to Panama. Juan Ponce de León explored Puerto Rico in 1508 and colonized it with settlers and livestock. He was instrumental in establishing settlements in Jamaica in 1509 and in Cuba in 1511. He traveled north exploring the Bahama Islands in 1513 and then sailed to the east coast of Florida.

In his explorations of Florida, de León was mainly seeking the mythical waters of youth which were later proven to be the artesian and sulphur springs found all over Florida which the natives used for internal and external medicinal purposes. He sailed completely around Florida, but savage natives prevented any attempt to colonize on the peninsula.

Vasco Núñez de Balboa explored the Isthmus of Darien and crossed to Panama and the Pacific Ocean in 1513. Hernández de Córdoba found the Yucatan peninsular in 1517. In 1518 Juan de Grijalva sailed the coast northward from Campeche to Tampico, Mexico. Hernán Cortés came to Mexico in 1519 and conquered Mexico City with the aid of about ten thousand disgruntled Aztecs who were angry with Montezuma. Alonso Alvarez de Pineda explored the Gulf coast from the mouth of the Mississippi to Tampico,

Mexico, in 1519. In 1523 Pedro de Alvarado led an overland expedition into Guatemala. Pánfilo de Narváez came to Florida in 1528 and Álvar Núñez Cabeza de Vaca explored Florida to Mexico, 1528-36.

In 1531 Spanish explorer Francisco Pizarro marched inland from Ecuador's coast and found the ancient Incan empire. They slaughtered, raped and plundered for the gold and silver of Peru. By 1535, Pizarro had founded Lima as his capital.

Hernando de Soto explored Florida and nine other southern states beginning in 1539.

There has never been a conquest like that of the Spaniards in the annals of the human race. In one generation, Spain through its conquistadors, had occupied more new territory than the Romans conquered in fifty years. Genghis Khan swept over a greater area, but left death and destruction in his wake; complete chaos lasted a century afterwards.

Within thirty-five years, Spanish conquistadors had cut a murderous swath from Mexico across South America, including all of Central America, with more to come. The motto of the conquistadors was "we come for the service of God and for Spain, and gold for ourselves."

The New World Expands

In 1512 the largest European colony in the New World was Santo Domingo, the capital of Hispaniola. It was a Spanish agricultural and mining colony producing cattle, hogs, goats, horses, cotton, sugar cane, copper, and, of course, gold. It was exporting nearly one million dollars in mined gold a year to Spain.

The Spanish conquistadors were brave and hardy beyond any question, but usually had a deep-seated distaste and even contempt for labor with their hands. To dig in the mines and do the many other sorts of menial work necessary to make the colonies profitable for the crown, they needed a large supply of laborers. The Spanish colonists thought their proper career was as soldier or administrator.

The Spaniard's mining operation had enslaved natives as forced labor, but since the natives were unaccustomed to such hard work they did not survive long in that unbearable environment. They were replaced by kidnapped

Spanish conquerors force native Americans to carry heavy loads in a Spanish pack train. Those who lag behind are put to the sword.

natives from other Caribbean Islands, Florida and the Bahamas, but they suffered the same fate. The Amerindians had no word in their language for "work"; their lifestyle had been free as the wild birds and animals which shared their simple life. They could not be regimented. In 1512 the first kidnapped Negro slaves were brought by the Portuguese from Africa to work the gold mines of Hispaniola. The "black gold" trade had begun in the New World and this opened the door for further piracy.

The clear blue-green waters of the Gulf of Mexico and the Caribbean Sea help form the Gulf Stream first observed and documented by Ponce de León. The stream is dotted with palm-fringed fertile islands with dense jungle and mangrove swamps and clean white beaches. Spain claimed all of them. To a great extent, Santo Domingo became the center from which the rest of the New World was explored, exploited and colonized. The more adventurous spirits of Hispaniola grew dissatisfied with the humdrum life of sugar and cotton plantations and overseeing the mines, so petty officials obtained royal licenses from Spain to conquer and colonize other islands. They were joined in their quest by other Spanish advancers who explored the nearby islands, but only the larger islands were colonized — Cuba, Puerto Rico, Hispaniola and Jamaica.

The Spanish Main

Within sixty years after Columbus' first voyage, the Spanish Empire had explored and conquered the northern and western part of South America (known as Tierra Firma), most of the islands of the Caribbean Sea, the republics known today as Central America, and all of Mexico. The mainland of Central America and the northern coast of South America was originally

designated the Spanish Main, but as Spanish colonies were established on the numerous Caribbean Islands and the West Indies, the whole area shared the name.

The Spaniards organized and administered all that they explored and conquered. They immediately brought from their motherland the arts and letters of Europe and where the sword went, the cross went also. They converted thousands of Amerindians to their Catholic faith as the Spaniards incorporated the natives into their society. The friars encouraged intermarriage of Europeans, American Indians and Negroes, creating a heterogeneous culture less marked by racial prejudice.

In Mexico, the Aztecs revealed their secret method of smelting silver in clay pots with air holes. Placing charcoal in the bottom of the clay pot, they inserted silver ore on top, placed jars on top of any high ridges, then set the charcoal on fire. Soon the pure silver poured out through the air holes. They re-smelted the silver into bars and stamped them with the king's seal. The bars were packed in skin sacks and thrown across the backs of packmules and native llamas to travel the sloping trails to the east

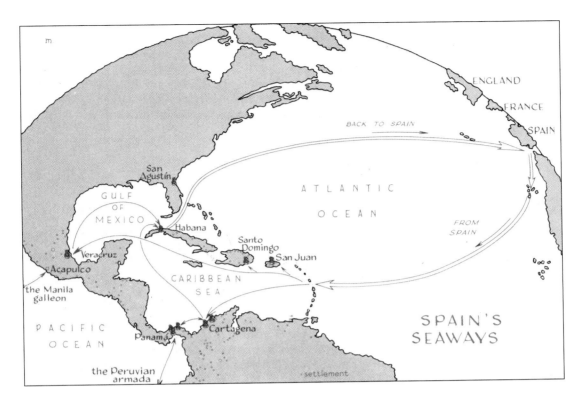

Map labels: ENGLAND, FRANCE, SPAIN, BACK TO SPAIN, ATLANTIC OCEAN, FROM SPAIN, San Agustín, GULF OF MEXICO, Habana, Santo Domingo, San Juan, Veracruz, Acapulco, the Manila galleon, CARIBBEAN SEA, SPAIN'S SEAWAYS, PACIFIC OCEAN, Panama, Cartagena, the Peruvian armada, settlement

coast for shipment to Spain. The beautiful golden statues of the gods of the Aztecs and Incas (of South America) were stolen and many melted down for transporting in gold bars back to Spain. The native Amerindians were forced to work the large silver and gold mines in Peru and Mexico and the lesser copper mines in Cuba and Hispaniola and the smaller islands in the Caribbean.

Mexico City and Lima, Peru, the cities of Indian kings, became seats of urban civilization within fifteen years of the conquests. The pagan temples were dismantled and in their place were built Catholic churches out of the same building stones, places of refuge and worship. The first printing press in the New World came by Spanish galleon to Mexico City in 1539 and in both Mexico City and Lima, a university was founded in 1551.

In the 1500s, religious antagonism ran rampant in Europe and also in the New World. The conflicts between Protestants and Catholics of Europe had significant bearing on all that happened in the Spanish Main. The appetites of England, France, Germany and the Netherlands was whetted to acquire colonial possessions of their own in the New World. These and other countries of Europe were not competitive since they did not have the naval strength, ships, nor money to finance such voyages and explorations. But they were steaming with jealousy and envy, and being mostly Protestant, were adamantly against the Pope for dividing up the New World for only Catholic Spain and Portugal.

Spain claimed ownership of all the lands they "discovered" for over a century after Columbus' first voyage. The Spaniards tried to deny the right of ships of other countries to enter the area, even for trade.

The Spaniards were aware of the large eastern coast of North America, but had virtually ignored it since there was found no great quantities of treasure in their initial explorations. With the exception of Florida, their interests lay in the riches of Central and South America and the Caribbean Islands. Although the natives there were more highly civilized and much more inclined to protect their land with warfare, the Spaniards considered the reward worth the risk.

However, other European explorers found the vast North American coast easier to approach since the natives were friendly and the land rich with opportunity for peaceful settlement. They also began to colonize the smaller islands overlooked by the Spaniards, thereby planting the seed of piracy.

The Spaniards considered themselves the protectors and promoters of Catholicism and originally did everything they could to assist their Catholic colonies in repelling the fast growing forces of Protestantism from England, France, Holland and Germany. These countries hated the covetous Spaniards who thought they owned most of the old world and by the act of "discovery," all of the New World.

Piracy existed in all parts of the early known world, but the Spanish-controlled New World held great fortunes which were flauntingly exposed when enormous cargos were carried across the Atlantic in Spanish ships. Naturally, the interest of pirates was drawn to the scene by the exploitation of the New World. Seamen on trade ships returning to Europe visited their old haunts and held their fellow drinkers in the taverns spellbound with tales of everything that was free in the New World.

Settling in the Caribbean, midway between North and South America, the privateers and pirates could plunder both ways. The treasure houses of the New World were now within their reach.

The French and English Privateers

Hernán Cortés opened Pandora's box with the loot he stole from the Aztecs in Mexico. In 1522, French corsair Jean Florin intercepted three Spanish homeward-bound treasure galleons off Cape St. Vincent in the Portuguese Azores, capturing their rich cargo from the Cortés expedition. One ship's manifest read: three cases of gold ingots, 500 pounds of gold dust, 680 pounds of pearls, chests of precious stones, lavish cloaks of tropical bird feathers, exquisite woven cloth, exotic animals and birds. The privateers had struck.

The treasure galleons which sailed back to Spain were heavily loaded and vulnerable to capture. The first targets of the French privateers in their swift sleek armed ships were single Spanish galleons. Corsair Florin played havoc with the Spaniards who did not think of themselves as pirates, forgetting they first stole the treasure from the natives.

Distressed by the costly French attacks, the Spaniards organized a fleet system, or *flota*, for protection. By 1526, all Spanish ships were required to travel in scheduled convoys. The convoys usually sailed from Spain

Ships in battle

twice a year (once in early spring and once in early fall) with new settlers, supplies and live stock for the New World. Each flota had a specific destination in the Caribbean to unload and then pick up the treasure from various ports in the Spanish colonies. The Manilla fleet brought fine china, porcelain and silk from the Philippines to Acapulco, then it was transported over land by packmule and slave to Vera Cruz, where it was picked up along with silver and gold from Mexico. The Tierra Firma fleet was loaded at Portobello and Cartegena with silver and gold which traveled overland by slave and llamas from Peru, Ecuador, Venezuela and Colombia. Copper from mines in Cuba was added in Havana.

When everything worked as planned, all fleets met in Havana in early summer to assemble the cargo for the long and risky return voyage to Spain, to refit the ships, and to replenish provisions of water and food. Large galleons carried the gold and silver, while the smaller merchant ships carried cargo of agricultural products and manufactured goods. Those arriving later spent the winter in Cuba and joined the next convoy to Spain.

An admiral was designated for the combined flota which would set sail for Spain with about one

hundred ships in a convoy, protected by well-armed galleons in front, at either side, and following closely in the rear. The protection given these convoys was costly and was covered by a tax on imports, sometimes as low as 6%, but at times as high as 40%. An official clerk accompanied each ship to assure the accuracy of the manifest for the tax collected in Spain.

From June to October, the Caribbean and South Atlantic were racked by hurricanes. If the convoy attempted to wait out the hurricane season in Havana, they risked sailing into the violent winter storms of the North Atlantic.

Spain's economy was strapped for cash; the cost of waging wars over their possessions and the extravagant lifestyle of the Royal Court, could not be met without the gold and silver arriving each year from the New World. It was essential that the convoys leave on time and safely transport the treasures to meet the financial needs of Spain.

French privateers waited in the Caribbean as the fat Spanish treasure galleons started sailing homeward. They spied on the route of return very carefully — north from Cuba, up through the Florida Straits between the Florida Keys and the Bahama Islands, sailing in the Gulf Stream close to the east coast of Florida (one of Spain's new possessions and as yet unoccupied by forts or colonists). The possibility of attack became slim for the French privateers, so in retaliation they started raiding ports, towns and harbors of the Spanish possessions.

Francois le Clerc, who was known as Peg-leg Clerc, commanded a group of a dozen French fighting ships, sacking first Havana and Santiago, Cuba, and then along northern Hispaniola hitting every Spanish ship or port in sight. Jacques Sores, wounded by the Spaniards in Havana, killed all the prisoners, burned the church and hospital and many homes.

John Hawkins was an English merchant and his three voyages to the Spanish Main were for illegal trading with the Spanish colonies. His first voyage was in 1562 to Guinea on the African Gold Coast where he bought three hundred Negro slaves. Sailing straight across the Atlantic to Hispaniola, he sold them for a great profit to sugar plantation owners. They wanted more slaves, so he went back to Africa for the second voyage with Queen Elizabeth's backing and use of a seven-hundred ton warship as the flagship of his fleet. The investors on this voyage were the Royal Navy Board and merchants of London. They brought four hundred Negro slaves this time.

Hawkins third voyage culminated in a bitterly fought battle near Vera Cruz which revealed the lengths the Spanish authorities would go to maintain their trading monopoly.

By 1564, after initial explorations along the Atlantic coasts, France was very much aware of the entire unoccupied east coast of Florida and the route of the return of the Spanish treasure galleons to Spain. France made a bold and arrogant move. Under the auspices of the king of France, a group of French *Huguenots* (protestants) led by René de Laudonniére, landed at the north side of the mouth of the St. Johns River as it empties into the Atlantic. There in the Spanish-claimed possession of Florida, they established a fortified French settlement known as Fort Caroline. This gave France a strategic seaport on the east coast of Florida to pick off the Spanish treasure galleons, and was convenient access to the inner territory of Florida as the south-to-north flowing St. Johns was nearly in the center of the new Spanish possession.

The Spaniards were quick to act against Fort Caroline in 1565. The monarchs sent Pedro

Menéndez de Avilés to Florida with 1,500 men and nineteen ships to capture and destroy Fort Caroline which he did with the help of a devastating hurricane. He expelled Laudonniére and his Huguenot colonists and established Spain's own settlement in St. Augustine, Florida's new capitol, south of the St. Johns River, making it the first permanent European settlement on the mainland of North America.

Within two years, Menéndez de Avilés also established garrisons and missions along the Atlantic coast north to Port Royal, South Carolina, and had traveled among the Indians in southern Florida and around the west coast of the state to Charlotte Harbor and Tampa Bay on the Gulf of Mexico. He had gone up the St. Johns River (traveling south) nearly to its source.

This kept Florida under Spanish control for nearly three hundred years. But during the years of the Spanish dominance in the New World few settlers came to Florida, and those who did soon withdrew as the natives remained too tough to conquer or civilize. Florida remained mostly a military outpost to the colonies of Mexico,

Central America and the islands of the Caribbean.

In 1572 Englishman Francis Drake told his men preparing to attack Nombre de Dios, "I have brought you to the Caribbean, the treasure house of the New World." This harbor near Panama was the main assembling point for the Spanish treasure galleons to meet with the mule trains coming from Peru and Ecuador with silver and gold. Drake captured in one single ambush over fifteen tons of Spanish gold and 100,000 pesos of silver.

Drake's second voyage around the world as a privateer was commissioned in 1577 by Queen Elizabeth I and he sailed for almost three years, the first Englishman to circumnavigate the world. In 1580 the gale winds of autumn carried them up the Thames River to Deptford, where a delighted Queen Elizabeth came aboard, dined with Drake, and knighted him on his beloved ship, the *Golden Hind*. Waterlogged, full of barnacles and eaten by teredo worms after her voyage around the world, she was laden with lucre stolen from a Spanish Peruvian treasure galleon and from exploits along the west coast of South America. The queen commanded preservation of the

Drake's Privateer "Golden Hind"

ship as a monument which lasted for one hundred years until it became so decayed that it was broken up for scrap in the reign of Charles II.

John Hawkins and Francis Drake were the two most famous English privateers of the 1500s. They were cousins and were both knighted by Queen Elizabeth. Although they were honored by English monarchy, they were considered pirates by the Spanish monarchy because the two stole from the Spaniards what they, in turn, had stolen from the Aztecs, Incas and other natives of the New World.

Attacks on Spain's American colonies were considered justified by her policy of exclusion, which other maritime nations viewed as an act of hostility. Spain attempted to enforce her ruling that no foreign ship should enter her colonial ports. Conflicts confirmed that peaceable trade with the Spanish was impossible and the only way England could get a share of the wealth of the New World was to use force and to plunder.

Spain's colonists pleaded for military protection, but Spain chose to concentrate on protecting her homebound treasure galleons. Battles continued throughout the sixteenth century between the English, Dutch and French against the Spanish, both on the sea and on land in the New World.

The End of the Spanish Empire

With the defeat of the Moors in 1492, Spain began a successful expansion of her empire from the Iberian peninsular. Her colonies in the New World had more than a century's head start on the English, French and the Dutch, and the stupendous fruits of their conquest, spiritually and materially, were the envy of all of Europe. Spain and Portugal ruled the world's oceans, harvesting without challenge the riches of their newly-explored lands.

In 1580 under Philip II, Spain conquered Portugal, uniting the two countries as one awesome empire — Spain reached her zenith in prestige and glory and became sole lord of the seas. The exploration and conquest of the New World with all of its riches encouraged and financed other conquests until by the mid 1600s, Spain's possessions stretched around the known world, one arm to the west coasts of Mexico and South America, the other to Manila in the Philippines. Spain ruled four of the six continents and every sea except for the Northern European coast and Africa's Mediterranean coast.

This dominance would extend for almost two hundred years. It began to erode as Portugal gained her independence in 1640 and Spain lost most of her European territories in the War of Spanish Succession (1713).

By the 1800s, the end of this vast monopoly by the Spanish Empire was near. Arrogant Spanish rule began to falter and fail. Dishonest officials, rampant bribery and the burning desire for independence lit the fires of revolution in nearly all the Spanish colonies in South America and the West Indies. The new South American countries had pirates of their own who quickly hit the Spanish cargo and treasure ships and helped to cripple her failing empire.

New World treasure financed unnecessary military campaigns for Spain; ruined her manufacturing efforts as industry was allowed to decline, exports decreased while imports increased; foreign debts mounted; and inflation became rampant, which finally led to stagnation and widespread poverty.

Her American colonies were filled with Spaniards who had an elitist contempt for menial labor, an exaggerated sense of personal honor, and an apathy for the royal authority which was absolute. Spain could not spread her defenses sufficiently to cover all of her colonies and to protect the cargo ships crossing the Atlantic with the treasures of the New World. The Spanish conquests were too swiftly acquired, too vast to protect, and too successful for Spain's health.

The Buccaneers of the Caribbean

The first pirates of the Caribbean were picturesque scoundrels who were known as buccaneers. During the seventeenth century, the buccaneers were the pirate kings of the Caribbean and stories of their adventures and buried treasure live on today. The term buccaneer has been misused many times to describe all pirates; the true buccaneers are the ones described here.

Many nationalities were represented in their numbers: English, Dutch, and some from Greece, Portugal, Italy, Africa and some native Americans. But the original buccaneers were mostly French, some were ex-privateers and seamen who had deserted their ships; some were criminals and rejects from society looking for a hideout; some were indentured French servants from the Spanish islands of the Antilles who had served their time; a few were young men of good families thirsting for adventure. They proclaimed their lot "a short life and a merry one!"

Originally the western side of Hispaniola and the island of Tortuga off its northern coast were the strongholds of the buccaneers. The Spaniards were a constant threat to the buccaneers' domain on Tortuga (Spanish for sea tortoise, as the island resembled a turtle shell when first sighted by Columbus). In 1654 Spanish naval forces devastated the original buccaneer settlement, but did not establish a guard force there to hold it . . . a bad move. Within a few years, the buccaneers regained control of Tortuga and the western half of Hispaniola. The buccaneer recognized no allegiance to any crown nor country, nor did he fit in as a family man; he was a loner

among loners. He would dress himself in layers of gorgeous finery when his purse was full of coins. He wore large solid gold earrings in his pierced ear lobes, he wore gold and silver bracelets, and adorned his neck with gold chains of intricate massive design. He was either very rich or very poor, but always his dress demanded his flamboyant bright red sash as his badge of courage, ever-present on land and sea. The sash could be used as a sling or carrying case for loot and held his villainous knife.

The buccaneer could be seen wandering the alleys and side streets of the semi-medieval colonies of the New World, swaggering among the soldiers, traders, Negroes, Indians, fair ladies, and the ever-present spies. His gold earrings, bracelets and chains were spent on pleasure and when gone, he was ready to go on the prowl again.

Since the Spanish colonized only the largest islands, the smaller islands were occupied by English, Dutch and French colonists, and even these changed hands many times through the years. The Caribbean colonies had no scruples against allowing the buccaneers to outfit with provisions or repair their ships in

their harbors; it was good business for everyone.

The colonies of Martinique, St. Thomas, Curacao, St. Christopher, Tortola, Barbados and other Leeward islands befriended and encouraged their lucrative trade.

The motherlands of France, England and the Netherlands found it was good policy to condone the buccaneers and winked at most of their life styles in their West Indies colonies. In 1666 the English Jamaican government listed in their minutes twelve good reasons for granting commissions to privateers whose ships were crewed by buccaneers, for the backwash gained the island necessary and luxury items at cheap rates. They brought gold, bullion, cacao, logwood, indigo,

The Boucaniers.

cochineal, and colored cloth from all points of the world. They also brought black African slaves to work the sugar, tobacco and pineapple plantations, and lastly, they were a rough-and-ready free naval force for protecting the islands from the Spaniards who feared and despised the vile buccaneers.

Peaceful Men

The buccaneers did not start out as pirates. They were originally peaceful Frenchmen who settled on the western side of the Spanish-held island of Hispaniola which was heavily populated by the Spanish colonists only on the eastern and southern coasts. About 1598 the buccaneers overcame the few Spaniards who settled on the island of Tortuga and established a colony and a fort at the harbor for protection from their Spanish neighbors on Hispaniola. The peaceful French colonists of Tortuga and Hispaniola were later drawn into piracy as a result of Spanish aggression.

They were loosely divided into three groups: first the *habitans*, the planters who farmed the island of Tortuga; second the *chasseurs*, the hunters of wild animals on Hispaniola; and third, the boat builders and seamen.

The habitans cleared land and planted beans, potatoes, cassava, maize, manioc, yams and tobacco for their own use and for trade. They learned many things from the friendly, shy, native Arawaks, including how to build a palm-thatched hut or *ajoupas* to live in near the beach. The natives made and gave them their only garden tool, a stout fire-hardened stick to hoe, plow and plant seeds in the rich soil. They showed them how to grow crops like theirs. They taught them how to make a beer or liquor from bananas and

Saxenbourg decouverte par Guillaume Schellinger l'an 1669.

potatoes, and flour for bread from the grated cassava root. They taught them which trees to use for medicine, which produced aromatic spices, which were poisonous, and interesting names like *gumbo limbo* (from which they got a strong resin), *machineel* (which was poisonous), and *lignum vitae* (a very hard wood).

The Arawaks helped them adapt to the bountiful supply of free food found on their island and the nearby islands of the Caribbean — seafood, turtles, land crabs, wild pigeons, iguanas, cabbage palm, cassava, and tropical fruit such as coconuts, guavas, mangos, breadfruit, bananas, oranges, papayas, pineapple and limes.

In addition to settlers, on Columbus' second voyage he had brought cattle, horses, pigs, sheep, goats and dogs from Spain to Hispaniola which had none prior to that time. Since the Spaniards preferred living in their colony of Santo Domingo, they let most of the livestock roam wild throughout the island where they quickly multiplied. The natives living in the hills recognized the wild boars and cattle as a new food

source and tended and tamed some of the horses and dogs which they learned could assist them in hunting the other animals. The Frenchmen also recognized another ample food supply on Hispaniola.

The Boucan

The native Arawaks taught the chasseurs to cut the meat of the bulls and cows into strips and cook it over a *boucan*, a rack of green hardwood erected over an open bed of hot coals and covered with palm fronds. This dried the meat while it cooked, thus preserving it for future use. The French hunters referred to themselves as *boucaniers*; the English equivalent was buccaneers — men who hunted and cooked strips of meat over open fires until it was dry (similar to today's beef jerky). The fires under the *boucans* were kept burning with any type of hardwood which gave off white smoke. They threw bones, scraps of meat and fat into the fire, causing the smoke to redden and season the meat.

The Encampments

The buccaneers camped on the rolling savannas of western Hispaniola, the second largest island in the Caribbean. The hunting forays were from outlying camps of usually ten to twelve men. They broke into pairs with a partner, a good friend for companionship and safety, as hunting wild animals was extremely dangerous. The buccaneers hunted with long flintlock rifles they brought from Nantes or Dieppe; the guns were capable of firing two or three lead balls like a shotgun. They carried their bed rolls over their shoulders bandolier style. They split their tent into two sections and each carried part along with their cooking utensils. They slept at the end of the day wherever they were.

Some of the chasseurs hunted the cattle, while others killed the dangerous wild boars and salted the fresh pork meat to preserve it for trade and sale.

Occasionally, Spanish patrols were also in the mountain ravines. The buccaneers then became the hunted and often they received reports that fellow chasseurs were found dead in their camps from Spanish weapons. The Spaniards caused them much trouble, but the Frenchmen always bounced back.

The sand gnats (no seeums), mosquitoes and white ants loved their presence as much as the Spaniards hated them. One buccaneer said mosquitoes "buzzed with a Spanish accent." Smoking smudge pots were used in their tents and soft branches were put under the pigskin sleeping bags to repel the insects. Sleeping outdoors was just barely tolerable.

Each buccaneer hunting group was accompanied by a pack of healthy, tame, but fierce mastiffs, an ancient breed of large dogs from Asia; the best and most experienced of their breed and very necessary in finding the hidden ravines where the wild cattle grazed and wild hogs foraged for food. Oftentimes, with the help of the dogs, many animals were killed with only a knife fending against the horned cattle and large tusked boars. Many buccaneers prided themselves in selling hides without any bullet holes — their trademark as a knife hunter.

The appearance of the buccaneer was ghastly — hairy, dirty and smelly because his personal habits were minimal, but they were strong, seasoned men. They shared their property with each other without question; shot and powder, a knife, a musket or spare clothing if needed. Even the rum of another was his and shared.

The buccaneers wore leather hats, peaked in front, made of cow hide and pants and aprons of heavy course canvas duck cloth called *osnaburg* imported from England. The men and women slaves who worked the fields of the plantations on the islands also wore the osnaburg clothing to protect themselves from the prickly cane and razor sharp spines of the pineapple. The buccaneers traded with the plantation owners, smoked meat for the cloth. The pantaloons and shirts the buccaneers made from this duck cloth were very durable and would even shed the blood of butchered animals.

They made a wide cowhide belt to hold their razor-sharp cleaning knives. Their cowhide boots came up to their knees as the countryside was very rough where they hunted.

The animals killed were transported back into camp where the mastiff dogs were constantly around the area awaiting the throw-a-way pieces of meat which they ravenously devoured in seconds. Almost every part of the animal was used. The hides had to be spread out, stretched with pegs, scraped, rubbed with the brain of the animal, and dried in the sunshine to cure. Tallow was also a by-product of their grisly work and was made from the fat scraped from the hide; it was used for preserving the ships' hull and for candles.

They had four items to take back to the coast — smoked beef, salted pork, hides and tallow — which they traded or sold to passing ships, plantation owners and villagers on other islands. Ship captains were anxious to trade their gold coins for the dried meat in one-hundred pound bundles, as it would keep without spoiling on long voyages, was nutritious and the flavor was delicious; and also for leather which was in great demand in Europe.

The third group, the seamen, made canoes by using fire to hollow single large tree trunks (taught to them by the natives), and built and maintained fast lateen-rigged boats (called "fly-boats") used to ferry chasseurs between Tortuga and Hispaniola.

The Restless Buccaneer

When the hunting season was over, buccaneers would sail their fly-boats north to the island of Tortuga, their main stronghold in the Caribbean. They traded their products for provisions of salt, sugar, tea, flour, yeast, whiskey, medicine, rum, tobacco, powder and lead. The rest of their time there was spent drinking, gambling and carousing in the taverns with women. Tortuga was the nearest island where women could be found since they were barred from Hispaniola camps to avoid problems. If any were caught hiding a woman in the camps, they were immediately excluded from the hunting tribe of chasseurs.

When the buccaneers had a supply of flavored meat built up and their provisions and wealth was low, they left their fort in the charge of half-breed Arawaks and went to sea. They sailed around their island seeking a Spanish prize to capture in revenge for the

Spanish efforts to oust them from Hispaniola. Tortuga's location between Cuba and Hispaniola commanded the important windward passage which the Spanish ships passed through on their voyage home to Spain. In the straight of the passage the trade winds blew in from the Atlantic Ocean during the day making it difficult for a ship to sail into the strong winds. Between dusk and dawn the winds changed direction and blew toward the Atlantic, so the Spanish vessels passed by Tortuga late in the day. With wind from their back, they could hopefully escape the hordes of pirates lurking about. The buccaneers used the same wind at their back to capture their prize.

Brothers of the Coast

About 1640, the buccaneers formed the Brothers of the Coast. Its members vowed to follow a strict code called the Custom of the Coast. The buccaneers were very democratic and the code distinctly specified rules for election of the ship's captain and officers, division of the booty, compensation for wounded or maimed crew members, as well as punishment for violation of the code.

The shares of the prize were specified by rank and position on the ship — from the captain, the quartermaster, the carpenter, shipwright, cook, surgeon, and the sail master, all the way to the boys on board who served as cabin and galley helpers or shot and powder monkeys.

After the money, the provisions and foodstuff was awarded. Crew members taken as part of the prize became slaves and these were also allotted as awards. They were either held for ransom or did work tasks ashore as slaves to the buccaneers.

The same law was used among these buccaneers as with other pirates who would later sail into the New World: "The fund of all the payments being the com-

Death – The price of the prize

mon stock of what was stolen by the whole expedition." *No prey — no pay.*

John Esquemeling was a young French doctor who sailed with buccaneers and diaried his adventures with them in <u>The Buccaneers of America</u> published in 1684. In all the buccaneer exploits, they followed the rules of the Brothers of the Coast, operating separately but cooperating with each other when on a voyage of prey or attacking a Spanish land site throughout the West Indies and ports of the Spanish Main.

The buccaneers were a band of men who had hunted and lived together for many years and among themselves they developed a bond of trust and kinship. "Among themselves they are very civil and charitable to each other. Insomuch that, if any wants what another has, with great liberality they give it one to another," stated Esquemeling.

Building a Reputation

The buccaneers' reputation gained world attention in 1665. Frenchman Pierre le Grand and his crew of twenty-eight fellow buccaneers sailed in their small Indian *piraqua* sailboat. All were tired and hungry as they had been at sea for

some time seeking a prize. Soon a small fleet of Spanish ships was spotted; one ship was having a hard time keeping up with the group. After nightfall, as the lone ship was trying to reach the Atlantic, le Grand made his move.

They agreed to sink their own small sailboat so they couldn't turn back. Silently, the little crew of buccaneers slipped under the stern of the majestic Spanish ship as their small boat slowly sank to the bottom. Barefoot, they climbed up the back of the stern castle, ran boldly into the captain's cabin with pistols and rifles cocked. The Spanish captain and his officers were playing cards when interrupted and the buccaneers took the prize without a bloody fight. The captain screamed "Jesus, bless us! Are these devils or what are they?" His thoughts: Who are these Frenchmen dropping out of the sky? Where did they come from? Where is their ship? How did they do this?

The buccaneers quickly took possession of the gun room and other important areas of the ship, killing all Spaniards who gave them any opposition. The captain and his remaining crew finally surrendered.

The news spread quickly to Tortuga and Hispaniola and other islands, and other buccaneers decided to try their hand in catching a prize. Within two years, over twenty buccaneer pirate ships and crews were in the plunder business, all fiercely independent and very democratic in their dealing with each other.

Returning to Tortuga

Due to the Spanish threat, the buccaneers kept a constant lookout in the tree tops of the island fort of Tortuga, looking south and east toward Hispaniola and other Spanish domains to protect their island stronghold.

History records one agile lookout named T. T. Thibodeaux, a well-known French buccaneer (whose descendants still carry the name in the islands). Arawaks crossing the channel were hired as spies to report to the fort information gained on the activities of their hated Spanish taskmasters.

Many times the natives brought wounded African slaves who managed to run away from the plantations. The favorite torture the Spaniards used on the nonconforming slaves was to bury them up to the neck and let vicious white ants finish them off.

Early one morning the fort had callers — Arawak spies carrying a native stretcher with a severely wounded large black man. He had been a slave driver or foreman on a sugarcane planta-

tion. It was his job to blow the conch shell to call the workers to the fields and watch over them all day. He was a trusted slave until one day the Spaniards caught him stealing extra food for his hungry family, beat him unmercifully and then buried him for the ants. The Arawak natives heard his mournful screams of pain and dug him out. His head and face were completely covered with ant bites and he could neither see nor speak. The French called him *le Grand Bleu*, or Big Blue.

He stayed at the buccaneer fort for several months while regaining his strength and was tended by the gentle Arawaks with native remedies. In gratitude to the buccaneers he pleaded to join their crew and be allowed to avenge his hatred for the Spaniards. Many tales were spread throughout the West Indies of the feats of courage, strength and fighting ability of this free giant former slave. Stripped to the waist exposing his huge blue-black torso, he fought alongside the buccaneers, always with his trusty conch shell horn and his "sharp bill" (a machete used to harvest sugar cane) which he wielded with deadly force. Upon boarding, he was usually leading the way fighting to be first behind the quartermaster. His place in pirate history will live forever.

Nearly every pirate hideout and port of call in the West Indies had a tale to tell about Big Blue. His reputation of courage spread throughout the plantations and encouraged the escape of many black slaves who headed for the coast of their island prisons and joined a buccaneer crew where they were always welcomed.

The French Solution

In 1664 the French colonies in the Caribbean formed the French West India Company, a group of merchants who had the job of securing French trading rights throughout the West Indies.

In 1665 Frenchman Bertrand d'Ogeron came to loosely rule Tortuga and western Hispaniola as governor. A good man for the job, he was known for his resourcefulness and leadership qualities; he had experience with the French marine regiment, was a former trader throughout the Spanish Main, and had been a buccaneer on Tortuga.

D'Ogeron found his subjects were scattered and resisting the control of the French West India Company as the buccaneers were accustomed to trading with the Dutch as well as the French. D'Ogeron knew as long as the buccaneers roamed freely on the islands, there was little hope of governing them. He devised a plan to get them to settle down — "I shall order chains from France for these rascals," he said.

In 1665 women were still scarce on the island of Tortuga. By command of the king of France and at the request of the governor, a shipload of women called the "French orphans" was sent from Paris under the sponsorship of Paris nuns who sent them with their blessing; many were prostitutes. The voyage was long and tiring, but the women arrived in good spirits. The buccaneers had loaded up their hides, tallow, smoked and salted meats and came to sell their wares at Tortuga. Knowing of the women, they actually bathed and wore clean clothes. They were advised beforehand that to get a woman, the king of France required they enter into a marriage contract — "no free milk from the cow". In French it sounds more romantic, *pas de lait gratuit de la vache*.

They paid a sum to the ship's captain and the friar who accompanied the "orphans" performed the marriages after hearing confession from the buccaneers.

The hardships of their lives were shared with their new brides and many adventurous couples agreed to cross the strait to Hispaniola and work the land, hoping to raise sugar cane, cacao, indigo and tobacco for export and to start a family. Soon laughing children could be heard over the hills and ravines. Hand in hand as husband and wife, they forgot their former way of life and turned into farming families whose descendants have helped populate the islands in the Caribbean Sea.

D'Ogeron managed to increase the number of *habitans* from about four hundred to over fifteen hundred by 1669. The French West India Company thrived as tobacco, cacao and sugarcane production had almost tripled. The buccaneers continued to use Tortuga as a base as

Groups of "French orphans" are being ferried to their vessel for transport to Tortuga, in a 17th century engraving entitled "The Sad Embarkation".

d'Ogeron had no garrison and welcomed their protection.

The blissful peace did not last long; the determined Spaniards were again on the prowl with their armed patrols. The French occupation of the coast of Hispaniola and the fort at Tortuga again fell to the Spanish troops, whose general allowed the buccaneer families and the small garrison to sail to St. Christopher for safety. Shortly the buccaneers regrouped and retook the island of Tortuga.

The Era of the Buccaneer

The buccaneers began a great era of piracy in the Caribbean which gave them a way of life better than most had experienced before and provided areas where they could seclude themselves in hidden harbors to strike quickly if a prize appeared on the horizon. No one has ever calculated the value of the treasures and cargo gained by piracy, but after the share out, the good times rolled. Most of their wealth went to cards, dice, rum and ladies of the night. "So what, when it is gone — back to the sea for more," they said. Memories of their distant homelands were faint, drifting further away after each voyage.

The buccaneers of the New World were more fortunate than most seamen because they sailed and operated in warmer climates, had access to a wealth of native food, and were generally accepted in the ports of the new colonies as they frequented the tropical Caribbean Islands, South and Central America, and the eastern coast of North America harboring the thirteen colonies.

The buccaneers had been tame traders earning a living by selling their smoked strips of meat to passing ships. But this rough life of piracy had attracted the scum of the Caribbean Islands, and towns as well as ships were plundered to supplement their living. The three major maritime powers whose foothold in the Caribbean was unsure, realized that by supporting the exploits of the buccaneers, they could only strengthen their own position at the expense of Spain. The particular Caribbean form of piracy known as buccaneering faded away when England, France and the Netherlands had their rights recognized by Spain in an agreement for peace in 1697. The buccaneers were broken up; some retired to plantation life while some took to piracy on their own account and were henceforth known as pirates, enemies of the human race.

Descendent of the early buccaneers

Neighbor to the New Colonies

Following the explorations of the Spanish conquistadors in the 1500s, Spain claimed *La Florida* — the entire coast of the Gulf of Mexico and the vast areas of the eastern coast of the Atlantic — land already occupied by Amerindians. St. Augustine, Spain's only North American colony, was established in 1565 confirming the claim; but without the riches found in Central and South America, no further efforts were made to conquer the natives in North America and colonize.

Later, explorers from other countries naturally ignored the claims of Spain when they found the beautiful and bountiful coast of North America. By 1607 St. Augustine became aware of an English settlement at Jamestown, Virginia, violating Spain's claim. Involved in wars with European rivals, Spain took no action against this violation. In 1668 a midnight raid on St. Augustine by an English pirate devastated the colony, killing many and looting and burning much of the settlement.

In 1670 the English threat came even nearer with their settlement in Charleston, South Carolina.

Finally, recognizing the vulnerability of St. Augustine and the English encroachment from the north, the Spanish monarch provided funds to begin construction of an impregnable stone fortress at St. Augustine which was begun in 1672. Constructed of heavy coquina blocks made from the abundant coquina shell on nearby Anastasia Island, gangs of Indian workmen and yokes of oxen labored for many years. The progress was slowed by want of funds, lack of commitment on the part of some government officials, and epidemics which thinned the labor force. By 1696 the walls of the massive structure were substantially complete and the fortress was named *Castillo de San Marcos,* Castle of St. Marks.

While the English occupied much of the eastern coast of the Atlantic and ventured south ever closer to St. Augustine, the French traders and explorers had traveled the Mississippi River and built forts. To counter the French threat to the Gulf coast of western Florida, Spaniards established a fort and settlement at Pensacola in 1698.

The late 1600s were turbulent years for Florida, the Atlantic and Gulf coasts and island villages. Pirates from the Caribbean, English and French privateers, and English-led Indians made many sacks and raids on Spanish forts as well as on each other and Indian villages. Spaniards countered with sacks and raids on the English and French settlements and forts of the Carolina Colony.

Pirate plunder was only valuable if its value could be realized and it could be sold or traded in a ready market. Pirates in England were hunted down, but in the islands of the Caribbean and in many of the early American colonial ports, pirates found protection, hospitality, provisions, dry docks for the repair of their ships, able-bodied crew members, counterfeit privateer commissions, and lastly, a ready, willing and appreciative market to buy their stolen treasures and cargo.

The circumstances which converted the early American colonist into pirate trader was the hated Navigation Acts passed by England's Parliament beginning in 1651, which affected commerce in their North American colonies. The intent was to protect the English sea trade from the very competitive Netherlands. The Acts created a monopoly by stating that exports from England could only be sold in British possessions and in turn, the colonists could buy only British products priced by British merchants and transported on British ships sailed by British subjects. Conversely, the products of the colonies could only be exported back to England and her possessions in the same manner.

Castillo de San Marcos

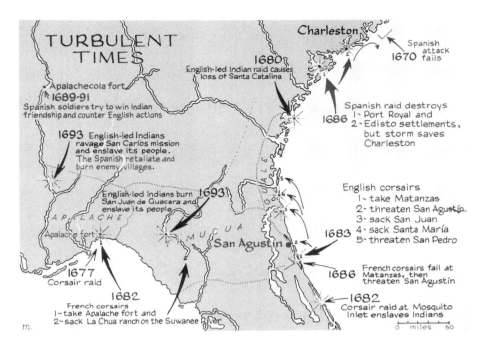

TURBULENT TIMES

Charleston

Spanish attack fails — 1670

1680 — English-led Indian raid causes loss of Santa Catalina

Apalachecola fort
1689-91 Spanish soldiers try to win Indian friendship and counter English actions

1693 English-led Indians ravage San Carlos mission and enslave its people. The Spanish retaliate and burn enemy villages.

English-led Indians burn San Juan de Guacara and enslave its people. 1693

APALACHE

MUCUA

GUALE

Apalache fort

1677 Corsair raid

San Agustín

1682 French corsairs 1-take Apalache fort and 2-sack La Chua ranch on the Suwanee River

Spanish raid destroys 1-Port Royal and 2-Edisto settlements, but storm saves Charleston — 1686

English corsairs
1-take Matanzas
2-threaten San Agustín
3-sack San Juan
4-sack Santa María
5-threaten San Pedro

1683

French corsairs fail at Matanzas, then threaten San Agustín — 1686

1682 Corsair raid at Mosquito Inlet enslaves Indians

0 miles 50

m.

The worst part of this one-sided British trade deal was many luxuries such as spices, silks, and perfumes were not available to the colonists as the prices were simply too high; buying and selling prices were set; and there was little demand for some of the exports of the colonies. This alone encouraged piracy and smuggling.

Pirate Dens

In 1655 England claimed Jamaica; the few Spanish colonists fled. With the French buccaneers headquartered on Tortuga, English and Dutch pirates settled in Port Royal, Jamaica. They were welcomed by the English authorities, for they would bring their treasure to Jamaica, sell cargo there for gold, spend their gold there, and help defend the island against the Spanish. As the pirates adopted Port Royal as their city of pleasure, it became one of the busiest, richest and most wicked ports in the Caribbean.

In late 1655, a London newspaper described Port Royal as the *outhouse of the world* in their editorials and drawings. They wrote, "The dump of all creation, unhealthy and more dangerous than the black death plague, as wicked and mean as Satan and hotter than hell." Port Royal, headquarters for most of the English and Dutch pirates, stayed as wicked as described until an earthquake in 1692 destroyed nearly two-thirds of the port and harbor. A tidal wave followed, killing people and animals and sweeping buildings and ships out to sea. It appeared as "God's vengeance for Port Royal's past wickedness through piracy" wrote an early historian.

The Port Royal pirates, forced out of their Jamaican den, dispersed among other Caribbean islands.

Fifty miles east of the peninsula of Spanish Florida, the Bahamas consist of over six hundred separate islands. The Bahama Islands were assigned by the English Crown to the Lord Proprietors of the Carolina Colony on the mainland of North America in 1670 with little remorse since the islands were under constant Spanish threat, most had poor rocky soil and they were plagued by hurricanes. The Bahamas are strategically located in the center of the trade routes linking the Spanish Main to Europe — a natural location for plundering pirates. One island in the Bahamas, New Providence, is twenty miles long by ten miles wide, with Nassau its only port. A deep channel harbor separates Hog Island (Paradise Beach) from the mainland, with an opening on both ends leading out into the blue-green Atlantic.

About 1700 pirate Captain Henry Jennings found a paradise in New Providence. The waters of its harbor were a perfect depth — too shallow for large men-of-war, but deep enough for the shallow-draft crafts favored by the pirates. High coral hills around the harbor allowed a bird's eye view of an approaching enemy or a potential prize. Natural resources abounded on the island; conch, lobster (crawfish), fish and turtles along the coast, and inland were freshwater springs, wild pigs, pigeons, bananas, mangos, papayas, crab apples, figs, limes and oranges.

Finding the island of New Providence to their liking and following the devastating earthquake at Port Royal, the Jamaican buccaneers moved their headquarters to New Providence. The Carolina Colony adopted a total live-and-let-live attitude toward the pirates living in and among the Bahamas, offering nothing and condemning nothing. Within a few years, a community thrived on the white sand beach island surrounded by clear water.

The steamy shanty town of Nassau had no law but the fist and cutlass. Pirates boozed, fought, gambled away fortunes, and generally debauched themselves, cut from the moorings of social constraint. It was said that when a pirate slept he did not dream that he had died and gone to heaven; he dreamed that he had once again returned to New Providence.

The vastness of the Bahamas offered safe areas to careen ships, to get fresh water, and for hiding places to sail in and out of to escape pursuit of the Royal Navy men-of-war. Their only neighbors in the Bahamas were a few remnants of English puritans who had started a colony on Eleuthera in 1648 and a few others on New Providence.

The nearness to the Florida peninsular brought the pirates to the east and west coasts for wood, water, and food bartered with the Amerindians, but only for these items as Florida at that time had few settlements for the pirates to sell their plunder, or to buy rum or supplies or spend their coins on women. And they certainly were not welcome in the Spanish settlement of St. Augustine!

Powerful England was concentrating her efforts against piracy in two locations. First, she confronted the pirates ravaging the American colonies by placing strong leaders to govern, and committing naval and financial support. At the same time, the British Navy stepped up their efforts to rid the island of Madagascar in the Indian Ocean and the seas around India, Arabia, the Red Sea countries, and the east coast of Africa of all pirate activities. This brought even more pirates to the islands of the

Small pirate shacks

Bahamas from their strongholds on Madagascar.

Then for over a decade, piracy seemingly disappeared as the pirates joined British or Spanish privateer crews participating in the War of Spanish Succession. With minimal risk and possibility of similar riches, most pirates took to the sea under the legal protection of countries involved in the War. Gainful employment offered them an opportunity to continue their plundering without risk of hanging as pirates.

At the end of the War, many young privateers knew no life but

the legal plundering of enemy shipping. Unemployment forced them into the illegal plundering of all shipping. With the new era of peace, many elected to follow the "sweet trade." Within two years of the War's end, thousands of ex-privateers, turned outright pirate.

By 1716 New Providence became even more lawless, vile and corrupt than Port Royal had been. The harbor of Nassau looked like a war zone, a shanty town of driftwood shacks and lean-tos with torn sails for doors and roofs thatched with coconut

---

War of Spanish Succession 1701-1713

By 1700, Spain had expanded her realm not only into the New World, but also had vast territories in France, the Netherlands, Italy and throughout Europe. Upon the death of Spain's King Charles II in 1700, French nobleman Philip V succeeded to the throne of Spain backed by France, Bavaria and Spain. England, the Netherlands, Italy and Austria favored Charles of Austria to become king of Spain.

War broke out in 1701 over the succession to the Spanish throne between these opposing countries of

Europe. England expanded the War by licensing privateers to plunder the seas against Spanish and French ships. Their colonies in America also supplied many privateer crews.

Between 1708 and 1713, privateers from England and the American colonies captured over 2,000 prizes — most of them French.

At the end of the War in 1713, Philip V remained on the throne, but Spain had lost her holdings in the Netherlands; France had suffered economically; and England was acknowledged as the dominant country of Europe.

On the prowl

palm fronds. Saloons, stores, and houses of ill repute were side by side, interlaced with driftwood and remnants of sunken or wrecked captured prizes.

The smell of the spent conchs and turtle shells drying in the sun, fish carcasses and crawfish heads mixed with garbage, and the stench of human waste could be detected far out at sea and black turkey vultures could be observed circling the island.

Small shacks were occupied by many old pirates who were alcoholics, had lost a leg, eye, hand, or arm, or were wounded such that they could no longer be a part of a crew. They tended small gardens and banana trees, fished and supplied some food items to the pirate ships in the harbor. Most of the pirate crews lived on board their ships while in port or many times just passed out drunk on the beach. The pirate captains of Nassau and their quartermasters formed a loose government, with each ship settling their own crew's disputes.

Loyalty to the brotherhood of pirates was higher than to any religion, race or former country. Their binding unusual creed was "enemies of the human race," especially against Spanish ships and their land possessions.

Most of the Nassau pirates sailed along the coast of the Atlantic watching the cargo ships traveling to and from Europe. Any ship was their prey. In his report to England in 1718 (based on information from his spies in the Bahamas), the Secretary of the Pennsylvania Colony estimated that over fifteen hundred pirates and their ships were cruising along the entire east coast from Florida to Maine, watching the ships in the Gulf Stream going to and from the West Indies.

Quoting Daniel Defoe: "The pirates in the West Indies and the Bahamas have been so formidable and numerous that they have interrupted the trade of Europe into these ports and our English merchants in particular have suffered more by their depredations than the united forces of France and Spain in the late War of Spanish Succession."

Piracy ran rampant during the eighteenth century, the pirates decrying themselves enemies of the world and declaring open war in the sea lanes of the world. They became a very powerful confederacy leading a lurid life style of independence like the world had never observed. Their trademark was their flag, a black Jolly Roger or the red flag of no

quarter, flying high on the mast-head of their evil ships. To avenge their lives against all the world they despised, they took to the sea which offered them an opportunity for freedom and possible wealth.

When the thirteen North American colonies won their independence from England in 1776, the complex system of trade changed between England, the colonies, and the islands of the Caribbean. The colonies despised the old English system and were tolerant with piracy and smuggling as it allowed free enterprise. The new nation of America agreed to continue to allow the pirates and smugglers access to their ports although they knew pirates could easily turn from a good-natured pack of scoundrels into a blood-thirsty mob.

The Slave Trade

The northern ports of America were closed to slave ships; however, the southern states needed the slave labor so their ports continued to welcome even the African slave trade.

The United States government passed a law in 1794 against American citizens selling slaves in foreign countries and in 1808 the law made it illegal to import new slaves to the United States. Smugglers continued to ignore the law and found plantations in the south willing to deal as the economy of these states was based on slave labor, an inhumane way of life.

Brothers Jean and Pierre Lafitte were Frenchmen from New Orleans smuggling "black gold" until 1821. Secure in their base in Barataria Bay (south of New Orleans), the brothers Lafitte sailed into the Caribbean and preyed on Spanish ships and slave ships supplying the West Indies. They sold their valuable cargo to Louisiana planters. A few smugglers persisted, however, until the Civil War. The last man convicted as a slave runner was captured in 1860.

A Band of Cutthroats

PIRATES

Their Life and Times

An historical scholar wrote that a pirate captain had the devil for a father and was suckled by a swine for a mother. Friend to no man. The privateer captain was the opposite; born and educated as a gentleman, he owned or captained ships with the legal blessing of his sovereign monarch or government. But their goal was the same!

The Noble Privateer

Every country in the world with a sea coast had pirates and privateers — usually at the same time. There was one vast difference between the privateer and the pirate. The pirate ship was an island of absolute democracy. Every man aboard had ownership of the ship and an equal vote in all that occurred. All spoke their opinions and the majority ruled. Each officer and crew member received a share of the loot. The captain served with absolute control only during the time of battle. At any other time, he served at the pleasure of the crew and with a majority vote, a new captain could stand on the quarterdeck.

Privateers were plain citizen seamen using privately owned armed ships commissioned by various governments or monarchs during time of war. The captain and his crew were issued Letters of Marque and Reprisal which authorized them to attack and capture ships and cargo of an enemy country.

The officers and crew were all paid a paltry wage and could be removed by the owners at will. Although a share of the prize was granted to the officers and crew, the greater portion was reserved for the owner of the ship or the government or monarch who sponsored the ship.

The privateers were simply legalized pirates in the employ of kings; there was a fine gray line between them. Privateer captains would resent this statement since they considered themselves in a lawful pursuit, honored by custom and sustained by profit. There was certainly noble calling in sailing in behalf of one's country for legitimate warfare. But many acts of theft and violence blamed on pirates were actually committed by so-called honorable men.

In 1273 the king of England is recorded as using the first privateer ship against the French. Merchant ships were used to trade goods with each other, but the early struggling medieval countries of Europe had no navies or fighting ships. Within the six hundred years when privateers were commonly recognized, there were hundreds of incidents of sea battles, fires and sinking of ships, marooning, thievery, shipwrecks, plunder, tales of horror, and feats of dishonor, disgrace and betrayal of men and countries. All were done by man, the crowning glory of

God's creation in days of long ago.

The Letters of Marque were supposed to end when the war against the enemy country ended, but many of the privateers kept right on attacking merchant ships. This made them legally pirates, and the warships of their own countries hunted them down.

One English admiral complained that "the conduct of all privateers is, as far as I have seen, so near piracy that I only wonder any civilized nation can allow them."

Author Alexander Winston in No Man Knows My Grave referred to the privateers as "the left hand of the king." They were charged with pursuing the enemy ship, overtaking it and claiming both the ship and its cargo for their country, and whatever it took to accomplish this was condoned.

"Whosoever commands the sea commands trade; whosoever commands the trade of the world commands the riches of the world, and consequently the world itself," stated Sir Walter Raleigh in the early 1600s. For centuries, his doctrine served as a virtual declaration of war on the high seas.

Many of the privateers were professional pirates in peacetime who were enlisted into the service of a belligerent nation as a convenience during time of war. One country's privateer was another country's pirate.

Crewmen of merchant or naval ships who were offered the opportunity to join a privateer crew, gladly did so. Although they found life on board ship no easier, cruel discipline was not practiced on privateer ships. They also knew the rule was "no prey, no pay", but at least they had the opportunity to share in the prosperity of a seized enemy prize and this attracted them.

During the heyday of privateers, the number of outright pirates who preyed on all shipping diminished.

Arrest of the pirates

War Over the New World

In the early 1500s, Spaniards had explored and claimed for Spain vast amounts of land in the New World. But Spain early encountered competition. France, the Netherlands and England would not concede that the Pope's openhanded concession to Spain and Portugal could shut them off from so rich a prize as the New World.

The seas were soon alive with privateers operating openly in the service of their respective sovereigns. This type of piracy was regarded as thoroughly honorable business. After all, it was war; Spain was conspiring against England; England, with inferior strength at the beginning, waged naval guerrilla warfare which finally wore down Spanish resistance. The northern European bold men who scuttled Spanish ships, murdered Spanish seamen, and ravaged Spanish ports were held in high regard by their kings. The French privateers began by seizing some of Cortés' ships in 1522 and continued their profitable assaults throughout the sixteenth century. The Spaniards failed to recognize the privateering commissions and claimed the right to hang privateers as pirates when they captured one of these independent operators.

The English did much bloody plundering during Queen Elizabeth's reign. Sir Francis Drake's winnings on one lucky raid amounted to several million dollars in gold and silver, plunder dutifully laid at the feet of his queen.

In the seventeenth century, Henry Morgan won fame and fortune as a privateer for the British in the West Indies. He overstepped his authority and invaded Spanish towns, villages and fortifications. He and his crews held the residents hostage until ransom was paid. They burned the towns and killed men, women, children, priests and nuns during the time of war between England and Spain, and he continued his activities when the war was over. The king knighted him. The spirited fights at sea served England well and embarrassed Spain. The Dutch and others also took a turn, but the English threat lasted longer and proved more costly than any other.

Closely related to the activities of privateers was the immense company of contraband traders who slipped in and out of Spanish ports selling their wares and taking on illicit cargo; their profitable enterprise continued throughout the colonial period.

During the War of Spanish Succession, English parliament authorized the use of privateers against the shipping of France and Spain. The privateers' method was exactly the same as the pirates — they approached a prize vessel, boarded and took possession of the cargo, and were not above violence and murder if met with resistance.

In 1708 English Parliament issued a law granting privateer ship owners and their crews all plunder taken with no part going to the crown. The intensity of privateering soared and so did the profit for captain and crew.

At the end of the War of Spanish Succession, the privateers crossed the gray line and became pirates overnight, often times stealing their own ship. During the 1700's, the uncertainties of island life in the West Indies included a communication gap. Wars often continued locally among the islanders long after a peace had been negotiated in Europe. There was rarely a year during that century that at least two of the European powers who had colonies in the Caribbean were not at war.

In 1863 the last privateering

The hemp collar

act recorded was during the Civil War. A Confederate privately-owned tugboat was licensed to attack Union shipping on the Carolina coast and eventually reached the Bahamas; it was scrapped for junk. Its part in privateering just barely made the history books.

Articles of Privateers

Examples of the contents of typical articles of a privateer ship:
- No ownership of ship by the crew
- No vote or voice in venture

- No prey, no pay
- Risk of combat, disability and death
- Shared rewards on a percentage basis:
  - Ship's owner received 50% of the plunder
  - The captain received three shares
  - Ranks below the captain received one and one-half shares
  - Cook's helpers and boys received one-half share
- A reward for the first man to sight a prize
- A reward for the first man to board the prize
- Fixed compensation for injury, disablement and dismemberment
- If captured by the enemy, Letters of Marque was his bail and bond (death by hanging was prevented, he became a prisoner of war and soon released)

Although the risk of adventure and death to the privateer was equal to that of the pirate for the same crime, the privateer was legally sanctioned by his government and considered an honorable man in the service of his country.

The pirate had no country and no loyalty except to himself. He certainly recognized the risk, but all of his efforts to take that which belonged to another was for his personal satisfaction and gain.

The Pirate's Way of Life

As an alternative to the horrible life of the poor of the day, many believed a life at sea to be preferable. But life of the ordinary seaman aboard a merchant ship or warship was not only no better than the poor man on land, it was usually worse. Once at sea, the sailor could not escape his servitude; he was constantly bound by the ship's rules; and his food, time and even his sleep was controlled.

On a naval ship, the ordinary seaman had no opportunity to advance to a higher rank, since only "gentlemen" qualified to serve as an officer. Although the seamen on a privateer ship were exposed to great danger in securing a prize, they received only a small share of the loot.

By contrast, every pirate ship was a floating island of absolute true democracy. The individual pirate placed the highest value on

his freedom and rights — and on those of his fellow pirate. This was the driving force that turned him onto the path of no return in the life of piracy.

The democratic pirate way of life allowed all to look and dress as they pleased. Rank and class distinction was nil. Respect was earned, not forced.

One noticeable characteristic of pirate life aboard ship was total absence of overbearing authority.

Officers wore no epaulets, stripes, or special hats or uniforms to remind them of the hated authoritative life they left behind.

Aboard ship they all ate the same food and drank the same rum and same water. There was no officers' mess, private cabins, special service, wines or privileges as was the custom on honest ships. The pirates even shared ownership of their ship. All had equal voice to be heard and an equal vote to cast by show of hands as to their captain, where they sailed, and when to board and fight for a prize. If there was a strong dissent of the minority, they left the ship, started their own crew, and set out on their destiny following the "sweet trade" in a new ship.

Although the **captain** of a pirate ship was elected by equal vote of all hands on board, he was not chosen on popularity. His elevation came about because he was respected, had leadership skills, bravery, boldness and cunning. He was "pistol proof": expert in ship handling, crew control and the tactics of naval warfare.

Pirate historian Daniel Defoe tells of the election of Bartholomew Roberts to captain where he decried his motto to be a "short life and a merry one!" The captain could be replaced at any time by another vote. Defoe describes this uncertain position as "a captain with a crew as captain over him and by vote could reduce him to crew in seconds." He also recounted that many captains kept their appointment for years, but one pirate ship had thirteen different captains within a few months.

The captain had total power of command only during battle when the crew had no vote against him.

The **quartermaster** was the counterbalance with the captain and he was also the ranking judicial officer enforcing all articles and laws. While major offenses were tried by pirate jury, minor infringements such as neglect of duty, abuse of equipment, fighting, or quarrelling were regulated by the quartermaster. He also conducted shipboard trials which were held to keep good order on the ship. All men were assigned as witnesses to beatings, public hangings and burials at sea.

The quartermaster, or number two man, was the trustee of the whole ship's company and even the captain could do nothing without the quartermaster's approval. It was the duty of the quartermaster to man the helm while approaching and overcoming the prize, and to lead the boarding party once the two ships were "married".

He was not only in charge of the pirate ship, but the prize ship as well. After the battle, he decided what plunder (other than obvious treasure of gold, silver and jewels) were to be hoisted over to the chaser vessel. His experienced eye chose the best of the loot to be taken to pirate brokers in friendly ports for sale. He also kept records of the acquired goods to see that every man received his fair share at the time of share out.

Like the captain, the quartermaster was subject to the will of the entire crew, selected by the majority of the crew, and could be voted out of office as easily as he was elected.

The **master gunner** was responsible for the care and cleaning of cannons and all weapons, training the gun crew, mustering the crew for action, and the inventory of gunpowder and shot.

The **sail maker**, **carpenter** and ship's **cook** were as necessary as the ship's **surgeon**. Each was a master with tools for specific jobs and was valued for the knowledge he possessed. Surgeons were always scarce and in constant demand. They were kept busy with amputations, dressing wounds, and treating disease. Tools were often borrowed, as the saw from the carpenter, or a pistol shot ball from the gunner so the victim could bite down on the lead ball during surgery. (So began the expression *bite the bullet*.) But his skills were useless against the frequent and contagious diseases common on the sailing ships of the tropic waters.

The **sailing master** was the navigator of the ship and responsible for setting the sails, checking all rigging and ropes, yardarms and masts for working order. He was in command of raising and lowering the sails, the flags and anchors, and sounding leads used to measure depth.

The **boatswain** was in charge of the provisions of water, food and rum; gunpowder and shot; the rigging and anchors; the ship's stores; and the maintenance of the ship. He issued his commands with a whistle which became known as the "bosun's pipe".

A Short Life and a Merry One!

Top to Bottom:
A curious Arabian stringed instrument played with a bow; a spinet made in Italy in the sixteenth century; a lyre made from a human skull, a rather horrifying instrument from Central Africa.

The **musicians** were popular among the crew as they played during communal meals, at time of boarding, to entertain the crew, and in battle. The music varied depending on the skill of the musicians and the instruments available to them. Most common were horns, drums, mouth harps, fiddles, castanets and cymbals. A lucky ship may have a Scot aboard who joined in with a bagpipe. Also, most welcome were an accordion, a lyre, a keyboard, and a conch shell horn. Sometimes instruments could be found gathered from all parts of the world — cowhide drums from Africa, dried gourd maracas from Cuba, bamboo drums from Hispaniola, flutes from Panama and Maracaibo and tambourines from Morocco.

Singers sang ballads of the sea and of their homelands, and the crew joined them in a familiar chorus. Lyrics were written embellishing the reputations of the captain and crew, the taking of a prize, the drinking of rum, and the wench in port; or laments on their life at sea.

While approaching and boarding a prize you heard marches, drum rolls, trumpet and bugle calls. Sometimes even the cook joined in by beating on his pots and pans with a large spoon. The noise added confusion to demoralize the victim; it caused panic on the prize while encouraging the pirate crew. The musicians never joined the boarding party; they stayed high on the chaser and played loudly. Called "musikers" by some crews, they were an assorted array of talented sea artists.

Articles of Agreement

Pirates hated the rules and authoritarians in the world from which they came, but in joining a pirate crew all agreed to sign and obey the rules or articles of agreement for the ship. Men would take a solemn oath on a Bible, or above two crossed pistols, or two crossed axes, or astride a cannon, or on a human skull; but from the captain down to the assistant cook, all had to put his mark that he would totally obey the ship's articles. Many signed inside a circle, a "one for all and all for one" theme, and the rules were strictly enforced.

The articles of a pirate ship were demanded by the most illiterate desperate man. Abandoning a society they feared and hated, they still used the example of the legal Letters of Marque drawn up by governments recognizing legal privateers. The pirates hoped that if caught, they may be saved from being hung by having these signed articles on board their ship. Every pirate ship had articles of agreement with only slight variations. They were used for over three hundred years to keep the crew in tow.

Excerpts from a typical Agreement, these were used by Captain Bartholomew Roberts for his crew:

- Every man shall have an equal vote on any and all matters.
- All loot and plunder acquired from the prize must be turned over to the company for sharing — any effort or attempt to defraud shall cause the man to be marooned or killed. If any man robs another of his share, he shall have his ears and nose slit and be put ashore where he shall endure hardships.
- No gaming for money with cards or dice.
- All lanterns and candles shall be put out at dark. (Crew members could drink, play music and talk above deck without light until dawn.)
- Each man must keep his weapons clean, sharp, loaded and ready for action.
- No women allowed to sail on board. If any man shall carry her to sea in disguise, he shall suffer death.
- For desertion of ship, quarters or stations in time of battle; penalty of death or marooning.
- No fighting among the crew.
- No crew member shall mention breaking up until each has an equal share of money.
- The captain and quartermaster shall each receive two shares of a prize, the master gunner and boatswain, one and one-half shares. All other officers, one and one-quarter shares.
- The musicians shall rest on Sunday; all other days by favour only.

Some articles included a reward of the best weapon for the first man to sight a prize. Most included the sentence for specific crimes.

tic Ocean

The West Indies

J.

cos Islands
J.

J.

rtue

spaniola

Santo Domingo

Mayaguez

San Juan

Puerto Rico

Virgin Islands

Calebra Is.

St. Thomas

St. John

Amagada Br.

Virgin Gorda
Tortola Br.

Anguilla ~ Br.

St. Martin Neth ~ Br.

St. Barthélemy Fr.

St. Croix

Saba
St. Eustatius
Nevis
St. Kitts
Redonda

Antigua ~ Br.
Montserrat ~ Br.

Guadeloupe
Fr. Pt. á Pitre
Marie Galante

Dominica ~ Br.
Roseau

Martinique
Fr.

Mt. Pelee
Fort de France

Castries

St. Lucia ~ Br.

St. Vincent
Kingston

Barbados
Br.
Bridgetown

Grenadine Is.

St. George

Grenada ~ Br.

Tobago

Port of Spain

Trinidad

Golfo de Venezuela

Oranjestad
Aruba
Neth.

Curacao
Neth.
Willemstad

Bonaire ~ Neth.

Peninsula
de Paraguana

Isla de Margarita

Isla ~ Tortuga

Maracaibo

Caracas

Venezuela

N.

W.

E.

S.

A Difference of Opinion
By Rick Reeves

Dead Men Tell No Tales
By Rick Reeves

An Elizabethan money chest, reputed to have belonged to Sir Francis Drake.

A chest dating from 1725, made of wrought iron, it weighs 200 pounds. When full of gold, it would have required four men to lift it. The front keyhole is false; the real one is hidden on the cover.

An elegant sixteenth century money box

Some articles included a form of insurance for those wounded in battle or in service of the pirate ship. One example of compensation for injury was listed as:
- 600 pieces of eight from the common prize for loss of the right arm
- 500 pieces of eight for loss of the left arm (most were right handed)
- 500 pieces of eight for loss of a leg
- 100 pieces of eight for loss of a finger
- 100 pieces of eight for the loss of an eye
- 1,000 pieces of eight for the loss of both eyes

Some even included compensation for the loss of a wooden leg or hand hook as these were hard to come by and a pirate already dependent on this aid from the loss of a limb or hand, was equally disabled.

Some included a provision for lifetime service with the ship's company as the injured man may choose such as cook, carpenter or sail maker where he would maintain his value to the crew and receive his share of a prize.

Life Aboard Ship

Although simple sailors all, they were seasoned men since many went to sea in their early teens and quickly learned the ship's vital signs and workings from the keel to the mast. Landlubbers, farmers, shopkeepers, blacksmiths and deadbeats were not found among pirates. Only seasoned sailors who loved ships and the sea need sign on via the articles of the pirates' ships as they sailed from port to port, prize to prize, and rum keg to rum keg.

There were a thousand reasons a man became a pirate; no two were alike. They came from various seafaring groups — volunteers from the captured crew of a prize, mutineers from honorable merchants' ships, runaway slaves, deserters from the navies of Europe, and surgeons, sail makers, cooks, musicians, and carpenters conscripted (when needed) on land and on sea. Linquists speaking multiple languages were always welcome as interpreters.

They may be murderers, thieves, the unemployed, the opportunist, the adventurer. Those with education became the captain of a ship, the surgeon, sail master, quartermaster or boatswain. Those with natural talent became carpenters, sail makers, cooks, gunners, coopers or musicians. But most were illiterate uncouth ordinary seamen.

The quartermaster read the articles of the ship to all recruits. Men of the sea stood out and answering a few questions was all that was needed to determine the decision. If they passed the scrutiny of the quartermaster, they became crew members after making their mark in the articles' circle.

Many notorious pirate captains had no difficulty in securing capable crews as there was keen competition to serve under a captain with a successful record.

The makeup of a pirate crew included many British seamen and officers. Considering the great extent of coastline in England, Wales, Scotland and Ireland, it is no wonder there were so many seafaring men from this area — an abundant source of recruits for the British Royal Navy and thus, pirate ships. Many of the Royal Navy's practices and rules naturally carried over to the pirate ships' articles and crew.

Many sailors in the Royal Navy had been gang pressed into service; many had been convicted of minor crimes and offered the navy as an alternative to prison. Wages were extremely low and much of the wage was taken as payment for provisions and clothing. Often the Royal Navy ships in port would not allow liberty for their men, but instead would bring prostitutes out by boat to entertain the sailors. But hard discipline and lack of sharing of the prize money to the satisfaction of the lowly seaman was the main point of discontent, desertion and mutiny. It's no wonder that many pirates who were formerly with the Royal Navy brought with them the rules, language and practices of their former life.

Boredom and melancholy were the unseen enemy of the pirates. They had only constant viewing of the endless sea, clouds and sky; days of dead calm and relentless sun beating down on

Sewing the Jolly Roger

designed. The black flag was intended to flatter the vanity and reputation of the captain, the ship and the crew, as in one glance the victim recognized the threat and danger. Quite often these characteristic emblems on a black background were no more than crude daubs of white, red and sometimes orange or yellow paint slashed across the dark fabric. Other common symbols were swords, the devil, bones or an entire skeleton, an hourglass (which meant that time was running out), a cutlass or two, or red hearts dripping with blood. All of these suggestive symbols were to indicate to their intended victims that life would be short if they chose to resist capture of their ship.

On many occasions the black flag actually enabled the pirates to capture a prize ship with little damage or injury. So it was that they flew their trademark flags, striking fear and spreading gruesome tales about themselves to gain a reputation of terror in seeking their plunder without risking a battle. It was said "a black flag was as good as fifty extra men on board a pirate ship".

Punishment of the Crew

Throughout Europe, the Renaissance (the fourteenth through sixteenth centuries) brought tremendous advancements in the arts — theater, literature, music, philosophy, sculpture, art, and in architecture and construction of beautiful massive cathedrals and public and private buildings. But the classes were extremely divided with the monarchs, gentry, members of court, landowners and leaders in industry and banking accumulating great wealth and social position, while the lower class continued to suffer poverty and injustice at the hand of the wealthy and powerful.

Punishment and torture common in the Middle Ages carried over into this period of cultural advancement. Particularly brutal was the legal torture common in prisons filled with men, women and children for even minor infractions of the law. Torture was used not only for a real or perceived crime, but for extracting information. The most severe punishment was for treason; for those who dared to oppose the will of the State. Accused as witches, many women faced the same torture.

A press was used to place weights on the torso of the prisoner until he or she was crushed or the warden was pleased with their suffering.

The thumb screw was common, as was branding on the face with a hot poker. Some were nailed through the ears to a pillory and stoned to death.

Torture was even applied to children whose only crime might be stealing bread or cheese when desperately hungry; women fared no better. Public executions by hanging were popular, creating festive occasions for the townspeople with feasting, drinking and merriment. The prisoner was usually tied to a tree and whipped, and then placed in a cart and hauled through the streets, ridiculed and tormented before being hung.

It was a period of gross social and economic injustice in which the lower class, whether landsmen or seamen, were considered little more than slaves to the higher class of gentry who enjoyed the elite life. Sailors and soldiers took the memories of this life of incredible hardship onto ships and into foreign battles. Much of this same type of punishment and torture was used by the officers of the merchant and naval ships to control the seamen. Sailors in the navies of England, France, Spain, Netherlands, and Portugal all suffered the same fate. It is no wonder that these punishments made sailors hate authority and *this hatred drew them to piracy more than any other force*.

In the New World, life was not

much better than in Europe. Convicts had been transported to the colonies as indentured servants; black slaves and displaced Indians all lived lives as bleak as the Europeans of that day. Spaniards used Indians to work their mines; French slave traders had no reluctance to separate family members to make a sale; British colonists favored the whipping post, stocks, the ducking stool and the gallows to enforce their laws. From this perspective, a life at sea seemed better than a life of toil on land.

Seamen were bound by the ship's articles and had no right to strike, but they had many grievances on the harsh discipline and punishment served to them as easy victims by cruel, sadistic, vengeful officers and power-bent captains.

Mutiny is the willful seditious act of rebellion against authority by sailors in port or on board merchant and naval ships. By refusing to obey orders, the penalty was death. But release from the confining and demeaning life as crew member aboard a merchant or naval ship made the risk worth the consequences since sometimes the mutineers were successful in securing the ship away from the officers and taking over control of their own destiny — unless caught, then certain death awaited them.

Many seamen disappeared into the life of a port when granted leave, never returning to their ship. But the sea being their whole life, they soon joined a passing pirate ship as crew. Although many pirates were deserters from the Dutch and French navies, more by far were from the British Royal Navy. Later, many came also from the thirteen American colonies.

The officers and crew of pirate ships remembered well their past experience with punishment and torture and naturally applied these, the only rules they knew, in their decisions regarding punishment for fellow crew members.

Flogging was a common punishment which reduced a man to an animal when the cat-o'-nine-tails was applied to a sailor's bare back while tied to the mast or wheel. The whip was made of a staff of nine single strands of rope gathered and wrapped to a handle, leaving about two feet of unwrapped strands, each tied three or four times into one-inch thick knots. The entire lash was coated with tar to preserve it from the results of its use.

A single blow would draw blood and repeated blows would take off skin, cutting into the back until the flesh looked like raw meat. A dozen lashes was considered tough punishment. The quartermaster administered the flogging, but only for a serious offense and after a majority vote of the crew.

Marooning was also common and a dreaded punishment which a pirate faced for a serious infraction of articles of the ship. An offender was put ashore on an island or deserted beach and left to die; only a few survived. The entire pirate crew witnessed the offender being put ashore, usually with his cutlass and loaded pistol to use when thirst, hunger and desolation overcame him. Some men were rescued by other ships in time, but most died alone in obscurity.

The greatest book on marooning was the fictional story of <u>Robinson Crusoe</u> by writer Daniel Defoe, which was based on the real marooned sailor Alexander Selkirk. Many an unfortunate pirate was also marooned, but never rescued as was Selkirk.

Keelhauling began as a form of severe punishment by the navy of the Netherlands for seamen convicted of a serious rule infraction. A rope would be looped and dropped from the bow to go under the ship. The seaman would be stripped to the waist, tied with one end of the rope by the wrists and the other end by the ankles. He would be hoisted up on one yardarm, dropped over one side and pulled completely under the ship to the other side. He was severely cut by the razor-sharp barnacle-encrusted bottom of the ship and usually quickly drowned. This inhumane practice followed the Dutch navy into the pirate world, but was used only for a serious offense. All hands were assembled to watch.

Hanging was a frequent consequence for serious crime both on board ship and on land. The *hemp collar* or *hemp halter* was very effective and easy to accomplish by use of a rope from the yardarm placed about the neck and then a support removed from under the feet of the victim.

Running the gauntlet - a convicted seaman was forced to run between a double line of his fellow shipmates who struck him with a piece of rope on his bare back as he passed down the line — as hard as the captain ordered. This form of punishment was outlawed in the Royal Navy in 1806.

Walking the plank appears to be a myth included only in fictional accounts of the sea by well-known storytellers. Barbados pirate Major Stede Bonnet was rumored to be the only pirate that ever used this form of punishment and forced a captive to walk blindfolded into the mouths of sharks. There are no other recorded occasions of having the accused walk a plank and drop into the sea to drown.

When a prize was captured, the offer to join the pirate crew was given to all and if the answer was "no", then the crew was told they were free to *walk home*. This is probably the origin of "walk the plank".

Crime and Punishment

Some of the recorded crimes and punishments for a pirate ship show the cruel carryover from the former merchant or naval ships, although since the pirate ship operated as a democracy, each crewman had equal vote in sentencing the guilty. Only a few defined crimes called for the death penalty. Here are some of the typical crimes and punishments.

Murder of one pirate by another was always a capital crime. Some pirate ships prescribed the following punishment: the victim and his murderer would be tied together face-to-face and thrown overboard. No trial was held!

Guilt of *cowardice* in battle usually drew the death penalty or marooning.

Robbing from another crew member was a serious offense and a common punishment was to have the nose and ears split and be placed on shore. The exiled crew member with these conspicuous symbols of dishonesty would encounter severe hardships. All valuables found aboard a prize had to be delivered to the quartermaster for sharing within the space of twenty-four hours — violation of this rule resulted in death.

Smoking a pipe without a cap, or carrying a lighted candle or oil lamp without a lantern case when descending into the hold of the ship was a serious offense. All pipes and lamps were extinguished at nightfall unless approved by the quartermaster for an emergency task. Even drinking after hours took place on the open deck in total darkness. The very fine serpentine black powder which seeped from the oaken barrels with rocking of the ship, was a great fire hazard. One tiny spark and *swoosh*. The penalty for causing a fire was lashes with the cat-o'-nine-tails or death.

Fighting among the crew resulted in severe punishment for both parties decided by the quartermaster and majority of the crew.

Gambling with dice, cards and put-and-take tops was forbidden on some pirate ships but not on others, as some captains realized it helped relieve monotony and ever-present boredom. But gambling also caused many arguments and death from daggers, cutlasses and pistols took their toll. The crime of cheating a fellow crew member in gaming was usually punished by flogging or running the gauntlet.

Quarrels were ended on shore by duel with sword or pistol. The quartermaster commanding, each man was placed back to back and on signal, they were to turn and fire immediately. If both missed their aim, their sword was to be used until the one drawing first blood was declared the victor.

Drunkenness was forbidden on ships of the Royal Navy, but mostly tolerated on pirate ships. Each crew member was provided all he could drink of the readily available grog or other alcoholic drink while on board ship so he was frequently drunk.

Each pirate was required to keep his pistols, cutlass and boarding axe in **readiness for action**; clean, primed and sharp. A penalty resulted when this rule was broken.

Absolutely **no women** were allowed among the ships crew. After seducing the fairer sex on shore, a man may be tempted to sneak her onto the ship in disguise. When caught, he was sentenced to death on the spot; no trial or appeal.

The life expectancy of pirates was extremely short. While the life on board a pirate ship was harsh and brutal, the life of their friends left on shore was, at times, even worse. Slum living, plagues and disease, starvation and serfdom, hard labor and low wages, and punishment for minor crimes was equally harsh and brutal.

Piracy was a heinous crime throughout the world and, once caught, punishable by hanging in public. But considering the alternatives of the day, one can almost sympathize with the pirate's risky choice to gain his freedom.

The Pirate Ship

The best pirate ship was a stolen one and pirates stole ships that quickly gave them power, maneuverability and speed.

Pirates did not have ships built for them — they simply acquired a new one when needed. Many were stolen in the waters off Europe and disappeared as they sailed to the West Indies.

Shipbuilding was a respected profession throughout Europe, requiring the best in design and construction. When the primary use was trade, the emphasis was on flotation and the seaworthiness of the structure itself. During a time of war, the emphasis changed to speed which brought about different types of sails and shapes. Later, with cannons brought on board, shipwrights had to find a way for weight to be distributed during both sailing and action.

Ships constructed for merchantmen had vast holds for cargo with little emphasis on defense. Ships commissioned by monarchs were highly decorative, while the man-of-war was a functional vessel designed for serious aggression and response. Sturdy ships were designed to be used in the seas and along the coasts of Europe, but even sturdier ships were required when distance was the goal. The pirates never had a ship built to their specifications, as most stolen ships could be modified to fit their primary need for speed and aggression.

The seventeenth and eighteenth century sailing vessel, ponderous and powerful yet seemingly light and graceful as it moved, all sails set to the lift of the wind and sea, was among man's most splendid creations.

The Pirates' Choice

The pirates preferred the three-masted square-rigger, the brigantine, the sloop, or the schooner. Although relatively slow, the square-rigger was chosen for long voyages. Two hundred twenty-five to three hundred fifty tons was large enough to accommodate two hundred crew members, have spacious cargo space for loot, and room to mount twenty to twenty-five cannons plus culverins.

The smaller brigantine, two-masted, eighty to one hundred feet, one hundred fifty to one hundred eighty tons, was a versatile ship which carried a crew of one hundred, carried ten to fifteen cannons and culverins, and was faster than the square rigger. It sailed at over twelve knots in a good sea breeze to escape any and all pursuers or to catch a prize.

Pirates liked the two-masted schooner because of her speed. The shallow draft enabled them to navigate shoal waters only five feet deep, to hide in shallow coves, and to sail at more than eleven knots in a stiff breeze when escaping pursuers. The schooner, up to one hundred tons, could carry a crew of seventy-five men, eight mounted cannons and four culverins.

The swift sloop was also used by pirates and smugglers. It had a bowsprit almost as long as the hull and maximum sails which gave an extra measure of speed exceeding eleven knots. It was not as shallow in draft as the schooner (it drew about eight feet of water). It could be as large as one hundred tons, carry up to seventy-five crewmen and fourteen cannons.

Pirate ships were usually stripped of all cabins above deck which added speed in sailing and outclassed trade-greedy cargo carriers (which were rarely fully armed with cannons since the weight of cannons meant less cargo). On the reverse side of the doubloon coin, the sleek pirate ships are shown as outclassed by the men-of-war of the Royal Navy, as the men-of-war were by the Navy's frigates and sloops. The pirates could only hope to outrun these sleek well-built vessels and avoid capture with their brave well-trained crews and *a little luck*.

With relatively new ships available to pirates through acquisition, the latest in navigational aids were acquired also. The compass had been somewhat improved by the 1700s and the telescope, barometer, sextant, chronometer and Beaufort scale were usually in use on stolen ships.

Many pirates were able to predict weather accurately and survive not only their hazardous trade but the sea — by observing the sky, direction of the wind, cloud formations and their height in the atmosphere, and other patterns of nature's phenomena.

St. Elmo's Fire

The masts of sailing ships act as an isolated point above the sea surface. When the electrical field is tense from the atmospheric pressure of storms, a glow of flashing blue-white, red and purple light appears as a dancing flame at the top of the mast. On board pirate ships it was a good omen and if double lights appeared, they believed a profitable prize awaited them. Some sailors believed it to be a forewarning of bad weather.

Columbus' logbook on his second voyage notes, "On Saturday at night the body of St. Elmo was seen, with seven lighted candles in the round top (crow's nest) and there followed mighty

rain and frightful thunder. The seamen affirm the lights to be the body of St. Elmo, and they sang litanies and prayers to him, looking upon it as most certain that in these storms when he appears, there can be no danger." Ferdinand Magellan wrote of it in his journal on his trip around the world.

The source of the holy "body of St. Elmo" came from a fourth century patron saint of Neapolitan sailors, Italian bishop St. Erasmus, whose name became corrupted to St. Elmo. The legend tells us that he was rescued from drowning by a brave sailor and as a reward promised to appear and display a warning light high in the rigging whenever a bad storm was approaching. The electrical voltage from this phenomenon is not considered dangerous. Sometimes it danced around the tallest crew member's head, yet there was only a tingling sensation. The pirates aboard their ships were fascinated with the bizarre eerie dancing light which resembled fire.

The Crow's Nest

In Genesis we are told, Noah's ark floated for one hundred fifty days in the flooded waters and then rested on a mountain peak. Noah opened a high window and let loose a raven to fly away in search of dry land; it did not return. He then let loose a dove and she returned with a green olive leaf which confirmed she had found dry land.

On early sailing vessels, a bird cage was mounted high up on the mast in which several land birds were kept: crows, doves, pigeons or ravens. If a strong wind or storm carried the ship out of sight of land, they would release a bird and follow his flight toward land. Even when the compass became available they kept the lookout on the tallest mast, and naturally continued to refer to the observation tower as the crow's nest. The pirates kept a man in the crow's nest who could sight a sail twenty miles away on a hunting voyage. He would call out "sail on the horizon" when prey was spotted, the war cry of their profession.

Enemy of the Ship

One of the enemies of the boatswain and his ship was the teredo, a sharp-toothed worm found in ships, piers, wharves and all wood submerged in saltwater. The teeth of the teredos grind night and day on a wooden ship's hull under the water line. Gnawing ravenously, this little worm has been accused of destroying as many sailing ships as have the pirates.

As early as 1400, seamen thought the worm came from the land by way of the timbers used in ship construction. In 1733 British scientist Godfrey Sellers proved the teredo was native to the sea, a bivalve mollusk.

The teredo enters into submerged wood in its larvae form, then grows rapidly into an elongated creature from one to three feet long and one-half inch in diameter. This was an enemy the pirates could not conquer. No wood has ever been found for shipbuilding that was safe from teredo worms. Honeycombed pieces of driftwood can still be collected on beaches worldwide.

Condition of the Ship

Ships which had been occupied by pirates for some time were very undesirable places to be. The crew worked only when something needed immediate attention. No unnecessary cleaning or swabbing the decks — to keep the ship seaworthy was the sole objective so as to catch the prize during the chase. Whether in port or careened on an island beach, maintenance was a must for pirate ships to enable them to chase and escape after boarding a prize.

Pirates were very vulnerable to attack when the ship was disabled for repair. Hidden rivers, cays and coves were chosen with great secrecy for careening. When the need arose, the ship was moved as close as possible to the shore at high tide and unloaded. As the tide receded, it was heaved over on its side by means of a block and tackle attached to stout trees on shore. All hands worked to scrape the barnacles from the bottom, replace planking infested by teredo worms, re-caulk seams, and put on a coat of tallow. The vessel was righted and refloated on an incoming tide.

Wooden sailing ships were dark, damp, filthy and gloomy, reeking with the stench of human waste mixed with stale bilge water. They leaked, no matter the weather; the pounding seas would gradually loosen the caulking of the planks. In stormy seas, the waves beat over the railing and down the hatches, washing the entire lower deck. Once the inside of the ship was wet, it was difficult to dry; mold quickly set in.

Housekeeping aboard a pirate ship was horrible and the personal habits of the men were no better — the men did not bathe nor change clothes during a voyage. They used the bowsprit to relieve themselves in good weather or a pot in a covered box below deck. Their urine was kept in oaken barrels and gave off an acrid stench. It was gathered and stored as it was necessary for sponging the cannons since salt water would corrode them and scarce fresh water was used only for drinking.

Often chickens, goats, turtles, or pigs were taken on board alive to be used as future food, adding to the filth and odor. Below deck was fumigated with pans of burning sulphur, pitch or limestone to stifle the stench. The accumulation of filth allowed vermin to breed in nooks and crannies which could never be thoroughly cleaned and dried. It made a breeding haven for beetles, rats, maggots, spiders, mosquitoes, roaches, and blue-tailed bottle flies.

The constant dampness and unsanitary condition of the ship greatly contributed to disease among the crew.

Excessive overcrowding was the worst fault of a pirate ship. To man the cannons and board the prize, the crew was three times the size of a merchant ship crew. They slept jammed side by side wherever space permitted. Lucky ones slept below deck in individual hammocks hung close together; the lapping of the waves lulled them to sleep. While some slept, others stood watch

Careening the ship

(although standing watch was often very slack except when the ship was on prowl for a prize).

The pirate ship was a means to an end. It was a working tool of the trade and necessary to catch a prize. If it became unseaworthy, they simply captured another ship and boarded over to it, sinking or burning the old pirate ship.

The use of cannons on sailing vessels, along with the ship's compass, and square-rigging of sails were three of the greatest discoveries in the advancement of naval power. These advancements assured the pirates' success also.

The Chase and the Prize

After sufficient time had been spent in a friendly port to repair the pirate ship, to have new seamen negotiate their status and sign the articles, to restock provisions of food and weapons, and allow the crew some time away from the ship (returning as sad dogs again), all were anxious to set sail in search of a prize. The hunger for easily-gained wealth and the thrill of potential crimes made all aboard the pirate ship excited to be under way. The goal of the chase on the open sea might be the prize ship itself, its cargo, its weapons, or the much desired gold or silver which was frequently on board.

The pirate's plan of attack on a potential prize was a well laid-out procedure. They would ply on all the sails for speed. The pirate ship would close the distance between themselves and the prize and would stalk the prize, observing carefully from the crow's nest and through the spyglass, the ship's length, number of masts, type of sails, rigging, its gunports and cannons, how low it sat in the water, the flag it flew to determine its country, an estimate of its crew size, the type and quantity of cargo, and how it was loaded (center, fore or aft). Often, if it were too great a risk, the crew would vote not to attack. If the pirates agreed to attack, they might stalk for days. The game would be like a cheetah chasing a gazelle in the vast open Serengeti plains of Africa.

Taking the Prize

Once all circumstances were in his favor, the pirate captain would order the crew to prepare to overtake the prize. If the pirate ship was in equal or better condition and the wind was right, the pirate ship could approach the prize prepared to board and conquer. If the pirate captain needed a new transport vessel for his crew or he wanted an additional vessel for his fleet, he would attempt to prevent any damage to the prize. Also, they could not risk sinking the prize with all her plunder!

In approaching the victim the pirates used an old trick. They ran a flag the same as that of the victim up the mast to get near without suspicion. The prize was approached slowly, creeping up to within cannon range; then they would strike their colors down and run up their own hideous black flag before the victim could realize the danger and protect itself.

The pirates tried every available scare tactic; they would run up on a prize with force, band playing, loud shouts, the black flag flying. Many times, the element of surprise combined with the quickness of the pirates in boarding and overcoming the crew was enough. To preserve the condition of the prize, the captain would have all cannons fire blanks broadside just for noise and panic effect. Many an accurate shot was fired across the bow of the intended prize and was at times enough to cease the chase and heave to for boarding.

Choices

On the open sea, after the captured ship was commandeered, the entire crew might transfer from the dirty, old pirate ship in a state of disrepair to the clean merchant ship, with better sails, new rigging and abundant stores of food and medicine. They would leave the cargo intact and head for the nearest port where they could fence the loot for cash, sometimes transferring the crew of the prize to the old pirate ship with no weapons or provisions and bid them *bon voyage*.

If their crew was large enough and the cargo tempting enough, or if the prize's captain resisted, they may split their own crew, take over the prize, and sail to a friendly port.

If their current pirate ship was large, powerful and in good condition, the pirates had no interest in the prize ship itself, and instead took whatever they wanted of the cargo along with weapons, gunpowder and provisions for their own ship. If there was no resistance to their plundering and thievery by the captain of the prize and his crew, they may be allowed to live and continue on their journey — minus their own provisions and weapons, of course.

If the cargo was their only goal and they had no need of the ship, the approach was entirely different. Accurate cannon fire into the enemy ship's rigging slowed the prize. Many lowered their colors as soon as the first shot was fired, especially merchant ships whose crew were low-paid ordinary sailors who had no

desire to risk their necks for a rich man's cargo or ship. Many ship owners gave advance orders to their captains not to resist the pirates, hoping to avoid death for its crew and save destruction of the ship. By threat of death, they became the pirate's partner.

The crew was offered the opportunity to join the pirate crew. Based solely on the pirate's reputation for vicious behavior, many crewman would offer to join the pirates to save their own lives. If they declined, they were subjected to the cruel torture given many victims after capture.

We listen as Captain Charles Bellamy dresses down a pompous captain of a captured fat merchantman who adamantly refused to join the pirate crew. In heated anger he turned to him and said, "Damn ye, you are a sneaking puppy, and so are all those others who will submit to be governed by laws which rich men have made for their own security, for the cowardly whelps have not the courage otherwise to defend what they get by their knavery. But damn ye altogether. Damn them for a pack of crafty rascals, and you, who serve them, for a parcel of chick-enhearted numbskulls. They vilify us, the scoundrels do, then there is only this difference, they rob the poor under the cover of law, forsooth, and we plunder the rich under the protection of our own courage; had ye not better make

Attack, grapple, board

yourself one of us than sneak after the arses of those villains for your employment?"

Sometimes the pirates would agree to take only what they wanted from the prize, leaving the prize ship intact and the captain and his crew unharmed. Good quarter, or mercy, was shown to any fellow sailor who called it, and if they cooperated and laid down their arms against the pirates, they were released and sent on their way. If the ship was in excellent condition and the pirates did not want it, it might be ransomed to its owner who would pay to have his ship returned.

When the captain of the prize ship was also the owner of the vessel, that merchant ship or slaver would put up a good fight and the pirates would drop off the chase and seek an easier victim. However fearsome, pirates tended to take the path of least resistance. There was always another prize ship waiting somewhere. It was rare that pirates were beaten off af-

ter attack. If they did engage in battle, they usually won.

The Attack

If the vessel attempted escape, cannons would belch a deadly warning shot across the bow. If this was not successful, the pirates would try to manage a better and closer position to allow the cannons to deliver a broadside blow. Often times only one cannon was loaded, but others along side it would fire blanks giving the sound of a terrific hit, spreading fear, panic and hysteria among the crew of the prize. If this taste of battle did not persuade the prize, a barrage of small iron missiles were fired from the cannons which entangled and destroyed the sails, spars and rigging which would then crash down to the decks, leaving the prize helpless and drifting aimlessly, allowing the pirates to grapple and board their victim.

The secret was in knowing when to fire the cannons. They were fired when the pirate ship was on the downward roll of the swells (so as to not shoot over the enemy ship) and when the enemy ship was rising on a swell that exposed below its water line.

If cannons were fired broadside, death came quickly as the bulkhead and railings were ripped, yardarms and masts fell, oak wood splinters splattered like small, sharp knives of steel piercing hands, chests, faces, and legs. No

part of the body escaped the wooden shrapnel missiles, leaving a deadly ghastly scene.

The attack was sometimes made from the ship's stern. The experienced helmsman of the pirate ship tried to keep his ship in the wake of the prize by exactly duplicating the set of their sails. His only concern was the cannons mounted in the aftercastle of the prize whose gunports could open and fire at the pirates.

As soon as the gunports were opened, they would receive volleys of rifle fire until the prize's cannons were silenced. Then the ruddermen moved forward with wedges and heavy oak mallets to grab the rudder of the prize ship and drive wooden wedges into the stern post, disabling the ship. Sharp grapple hooks were attached to the prize which held the two ships close together. The two ships were "married" as pirates securely lashed them together to keep from drifting apart. The prize would be helplessly floundering and its sails flapping and jerking. The order was heard to begin boarding and the battle was on!

As the pirates boarded, hand-to-hand combat was fought in shrouds of gun smoke, confusion and deafening noise. The pirates were often barefoot. Many were bare to the waist and dressed in short canvas pants held up with wide leather belts holding their

Iron missiles

shot and powder. They clamored aboard their prize clinging to the grapple ropes held fast to the ornate scroll design on the aftercastle, their bare toes seeking room to climb, knocking out the rear windows of the captain's main cabin and entering there.

Other tactics used to overcome the crew of the prize included throwing sulphur and lime on the prize's crew; and preparing and throwing "stink pots" and hand grenades, deadly missiles of death.

Fate of the Victims

The captain of the prize and those of his crew who chose not to join the ranks of the pirates were disposed of, their fate determined by the pirate crew and its mood of the day. They might run the men around and around the deck until they collapsed. Some were stripped of all clothes, their privates parts cut off as were their hands and arms. They were pulled behind the ship by their feet, or hung from the yardarms for crew target practice with pistols and muskets. Many were thrown overboard to drown, some with their stomachs cut open so they would sink faster. Others were stripped naked and put ashore on an uninhabited island without provisions, weapons or hope of being rescued, or were put in a lifeboat and pointed toward the nearest land. Many captured were beaten with the cat's tails or were keel-

hauled. Invariably, female captives were raped.

Marco Polo (1254-1324) told of his encounter with pirates of the most desperate character who when they seized a traveling merchant ship, immediately forced the captain to drink a quantity of sea water which would either cause immediate vomiting or would serve as a laxative. This enabled the pirates to discover if any jewels or pearls were swallowed upon the approach of their raiding ship. This procedure was fairly standard in piracy.

Freedom was only one of the attributes to call a man to piracy; the other was vengeance and hatred against the society that saddled him with laws and authority. When boarding a prize the captain and officers were targeted for death first, representing images from the past. At times, the pirates would tie the captain of the prize to his own mast and question his crew as to whether he was a good captain or a bad one. If the answer was that he was a bad captain, any number of torturous acts would begin. The cat's tails might be applied, striking his back hard and fast a dozen or so times, drawing blood, or he might be tied with ropes and thrown overboard to drown.

Other officers were treated as badly; many of them were tied by the neck or ankles and raised and lowered from the yardarms into the

sea. Many were set afire; gun powder was placed in their mouth and fired. Many were shot point blank with cannon fire. No torture was too severe for any of the representatives of authority of a captured ship or the crew who declined to join them — death and overboard for most, as *dead men tell no tales.*

The exploits of privateer Captain Kidd (who later crossed the line to outright pirate), strung up an entire captured prize crew by their thumbs in a blazing tropical sun until they told in blubbering sounds the location of their gold.

In the minds of the demented pirates, these men they tortured were old guards at prisons where they had served time; the hated judges they remembered; the sheriff of their home town; rich men in carriages who splashed mud on them in the streets of Bristol, London and Paris; landlords who cheated them after working them from morning until night; all the people who ever offended or harmed them were these victims; and the faces were many and the tortures severe.

The Catholic clergy who were found aboard Spanish prize ships were often brutally tortured because they reflected the hated Spanish and Portuguese crowns and their mysterious religion,

Catholicism. Many pirate ships carried vengeance and violence in their names: Death, Torture, Murder, the Hook, the Iron Maiden, The Noose, The Hangman, The Sword, The Twin Cannons, The Dragon, The Serpent, The Wolf, The Scorpion, The Strike, Viper.

There were times when the pirates did not capture their prize and were severely defeated. Even with their rapid sneaky attacks, some times they became the victims and were captured and hung on the spot, their ship sunk with no survivors to tell the tale.

The Bounty of the Prize

Common on the merchant ships traveling between the New World and the European countries were spices, animals, rum, indigo, tobacco, sugar, flour, hard wood, gold, silver, copper, jewels, silks and other cloth, medicine, housewares, farm implements — commodities that were sent from their source destined to fill the needs or wants at the other end of the journey. The cargo of the merchant ship represented a large investment for the ship's owner, and the captain was charged with its protection and safe delivery. But the captain had to deal with the weather, his sometimes unruly crew, and worst of all, the threat of pirates . . . the dreaded opponent.

Gold and silver were the most treasured booty found on any prize; it could be divided and spent easily. Spanish gold doubloons and silver pieces of eight were often cut in half or quartered to make legal tender for trade and spending by the pirates ashore. Cob coins were irregularly shaped silver coins of various worth hastily cut from elongated newly-mined silver bars, heated and stamped with Spanish royal arms and called *cabo de barra* or cut from a bar. Cob coins were sent from the New World to Europe and were used as common currency by many countries.

Crusadoes from Portugal, English gold guineas, and French coins were highly desired by pirates.

Slaves were often part of the pirate loot. The slave ships were chased and captured as quickly as a fat merchant ship. After boarding, the pirates often offered any slave a chance to join their crew. The pirate captain and quartermaster might strike a deal of ransom for the slaves or turn them loose. The pirates did not want to feed and care for either prisoners or the human misery found on the slave ships. When no ransom could be negotiated, many pirates would turn the slave ship over to the slaves themselves after killing the captain and crew of the prize, point the slave crew toward land, and set them off on a freedom journey of fair sailing.

Sharing the Loot

Different terms have been applied by historians regarding the prize's bounty — loot, swag, strike, treasure, lucre, plunder, booty. Whatever the pirate crew called it, the value to them was great — even worth dying for — and rules were established in the ship's articles for the award of the prize's bounty and carefully

followed.

Every pirate was granted an equal entitlement to fresh provisions and strong drink captured from the prize. Every crewman was also entitled to receive a shift of clothing, over and above his share of money. The shares could be in money, jewels, weapons or the proceeds from the sale of cargo from the merchant ship, but a share of the loot was given to all according to their own law of distribution.

Except for food, drink and clothes acquired from a prize, the quartermaster was responsible for the safekeeping of all items until share out which usually occurred on land after a successful venture and capture of a prize.

Pirates were prone to steal while on land as quickly as while at sea. Coastal villages and towns were not safe from them; they ransacked and burglarized peaceful people for food, medicine, weapons and anything of value which could be used or sold. They attacked the forts and strongholds of the Spaniards along the Spanish Main, burning their colonies and taking the treasures from their storehouses. The Caribbean was a chess board of death and destruction.

quences.

The myth of buried treasure has haunted men for centuries. Although there have been many stories of treasure which was buried by pirates on deserted islands and beaches, none are known to have ever been proven. Treasure maps have been claimed as authentic and sold in clandestine meetings to gullible believers as superstition plays an important part in these stories. Since the islands in the Caribbean and the coasts of the Spanish Main were known to all of the pirates, it would seem reasonable that if treasure was buried, another pirate would have found it before long. Also, a drunken pirate talking freely among his peers would have given away his secret. There are no records of discovery of buried treasure chests.

No authentic pirate treasure map has ever been found. Pirates were pleasure hungry and spent their fortunes on every whim, wine, women and gambling. *Easy come, easy go!*

Real Treasure

Real treasure exists, however, in the form of wrecked ships whose cargo could be identified and recovered. These treasures are generally the wealth of Spanish ships transporting large cargos back to Spain rather than pirate ships. Salt water has proven to have no effect on the quality of gold, silver and precious jewels and when found, they are as pure and beautiful as when they sank beneath the seas.

Weather prediction was certainly not an exact science and thunderstorms and hurricanes are common in the waters off the Atlantic coast, Gulf of Mexico and the Caribbean Sea. Even with experienced seamen like the Spaniards, the suddenness and ferocity of these storms caught many fleets by surprise with devastating results.

The salvage business began with the early settlers on the islands of the Caribbean who were

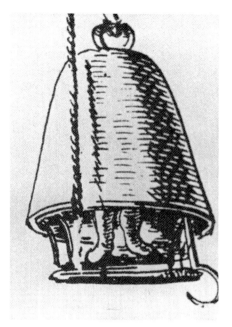

17th century Spanish diving bell

aware of the ships which wrecked during storms, many times blown onto the treacherous coral reefs just off shore. With primitive diving apparatus, they managed to recover great quantities of the cargo from wrecked ships.

Key West was but a spit of land until the 1780s; its place in history was in the unscrupulous but prosperous wrecking business. Fake lights and bonfires were used to confuse sailing ships, causing them to wreck on the reefs of the Straights of Florida funneling the Gulf Stream north to the Atlantic sea lanes to Europe. Most wrecks, however, were simply recorded as lost and lay buried under the sea for centuries.

Historical knowledge and research into Spain's archives in Seville confirms her frequent and substantial losses during the three centuries she was most active in the exploitation of the New World. Manifests of each ship whets the salvor's appetite making the risk seem inconsequential compared to the potential reward.

In modern times, with extensive financial backing, treasure hunters abound who risk their lives and reputation to dive to the bottom of the sea to search for

sunken treasure. Well-known salvor Mel Fisher, working with Kip Wagner in 1964, found one such wreck off the coast of Vero Beach from which they harvested over $6.5 million in gold doubloons, gold disks, precious jewels and silver coins. Did he take this wealth and retire? Certainly not; it only whetted his appetite for more.

Fisher's next goal was the *Nuestra Señora de Atocha*, a Spanish galleon en route from Cuba to Spain which sunk off the Florida Keys in a 1622 hurricane. He searched for sixteen years, spent untold millions in the search and finally, in 1985, found his *Atocha* off the Marquesas Keys between Key West and Dry Tortugas. He puts the value at $400 million and the *Atocha* is still not empty. Beautiful, deep green emeralds are still being gathered.

Other wrecks found by Fisher and his crews while searching for the *Atocha* are now being worked by subcontractors. The *Santa Margarita*, sister ship to the *Atocha*, is estimated to include a mother lode of fifty tons of treasure. (See inside back cover for treasures from the Mel Fisher collection.)

Another well-known salvor, Edward B. "Teddy" Tucker, is a native Bermudian. He has a remarkable record of recoveries and his unusual finds are impressive. He has full wine bottles from 1838, ancient Aztec axes, an Incan jadeite knife, a black palmwood Carib spear, and a 16th century Chinese pepper jar which came from a ship wrecked in 1621. He found the first piece of the jar in 1955 and the last in 1993!

Other salvors have spent their lives and fortunes searching for just one more wreck. One stated, "Gold gets you. It's the treasure bug — an addiction. Treasure hunting is the kind of thing you dream about when you're a kid, and there's a kid in everybody."

Along with treasures left behind in these wrecked ships, information obtained through nautical archaeology has provided a greater understanding of these ships and weaponry on board.

Commercial salvors today are accused by governmental agencies and universities of destroying the archaeological value of the wrecks. But the salvors have or are able to secure the funding required for the costly technological equipment and manpower necessary to explore underwater depths, where this may not be a high priority with government or academia.

In the meantime, salvors continue their exciting, dangerous and sometimes rewarding search for the centuries old treasures which still abound off the coasts of Florida, the West Indies, the Bahamas, South and Central America and Mexico. They also freely share information on their findings with nautical archaeologists, their investors and the public. Nothing short of restrictive law can stop them.

Pounded by a following sea, the great foresail broken loose, the desperate helmsman fighting to keep afloat, the vicious winds howling and increasing to hurricane strength, the threat of destruction to the ship and the loss of lives for the men is imminent. She sinks to the bottom of the sea, there to be battered about by ocean currents and partially hidden by shifting sands. Bones and timbers disintegrate, leaving only her brass cannons and precious cargo on the ocean floor. The treasures intended for the Spanish monarchs and their economy will safely slumber in her submerged bed for over three hundred years until another kind of explorer, the salvor, locates her treasure.

Drawn by the romance of the high seas, the drama of an ancient tragedy and the fever of treasure hunting, many will seek her gold, silver and jewels ... *but maybe her hiding place will remain secret forever.*

A Lasting Effect

The influence of piracy on the course of history is dramatic. When the islands were settled in the Mediterranean, Indian Ocean, North Seas, and the Caribbean, and the new countries of North and South America were formed, the pirates were there! The thirteen original American Colonies were heavily influenced and involved in piracy. The nations of England, France, Spain, Portugal, Germany and the Netherlands all were affected in their growth and the sustaining power of their government for more than five hundred years by acts of piracy through vikings, buccaneers, pirates, corsairs, privateers, freebooters, sea rovers, *flibustiers*, and sea dogs.

Roman lawyer Cicero coined the definition of pirates as *hostes humani generi*, enemies of the human race. Pirates unleashed their fury against the world and every ship was fair game. Their thrust was so powerful that the impact was devastating. The pirates and their gruesome deeds made them legends in their own lifetimes.

Piracy was virtually eliminated from the New World by 1830, but the dastardly deeds and infamous colorful repulsions thrived in years to come — the pirate legends would not die.

Despite their exploits in the civilized world, the pirates have been portrayed as heroes in theater, fiction, opera, poetry, film, and ballads; their ravaging and cruelty was almost forgotten as they became popular subjects of art and literature.

We all love to read the glamorous tales of piracy. The immortal Treasure Island was written by Robert Louis Stevenson to entertain his stepson. The Gold Bug by Edgar Allen Poe is classic literature. Noted author Harriet Beecher Stow (who is better known for her immortal Uncle Tom's Cabin) used her talent in a gory pirate's tale, "Captain Kidd's Money," published in the Atlantic Monthly in 1870.

Daniel Defoe's strange fictional adventure of Robinson Crusoe was based on a real-life story and published in 1719. Scotsman Alexander Selkirk was engaged in buccaneering exploits in the South Seas and because of trouble with the ship's captain, was put ashore at his own request on the Juan Fernández Island off the coast of Chile in 1704. The island was a water stop for sailing vessels going around Cape Horn from the Atlantic to the Pacific.

Alexander Selkirk was rescued over four years later by privateer Captain Woodes Rogers who stopped to fill his water kegs and secure fire wood. Captain Rogers took him aboard and in interviewing him for the record of the ship's log, heard the fascinating story of his marooning. When Captain Rogers returned to England, a local London paper carried a lead story on Selkirk. Daniel Defoe picked up on it and wrote the fictitious novel Robinson Crusoe.

Defoe lived with the early pirates in the 1700s and documented their dastardly deeds in his A General History of the Pyrates. An unknown artist's wood-

cuts were included, showing what these rogues looked like. The pirates carried no historians aboard their vessels. What is known of them has to be from the recollection of pardoned pirates, naval officers' logs, trial dockets, gallows confessions, and terrifying episodes from former victims who were set adrift, marooned or luckily escaped. Many times the horror and gore increased every time the tales were retold.

As early as 1800, pirates were portrayed in the theater as exciting adventurers rather than the rough gang of scoundrels they actually were.

The spirited, light operetta *The Pirates of Penzance* by Gilbert and Sullivan was first produced in 1879; filled with gaily dressed pirates, it is still produced by high school actors/musicians.

World-renowned pirate buff Howard Pyle produced sketches and paintings of buccaneers with their prominent bright red sash, their badge of courage. He illustrated much of the pirate lore written in the early 1920s and his art is still widely recognized and used today. Other artists have vividly illustrated posters, books, and magazines, and many fine works are displayed in the world's art galleries allowing patrons to marvel and relive the tales of piracy. Pirates are a favorite art subject — the more unkept and raunchy the better — with a wooden peg-leg, a hook for a hand and a patch over one eye for emphasis!

Robert Louis Stevenson also adapted and made well-known part of a pirate song:

Fifteen men on the dead
     man's chest —
Yo-ho-ho and a bottle of rum!
Drink and the devil had done
     for the rest —
Yo-ho-ho and a bottle of rum!

The meaning of the "dead man's chest" can be found in the museum of St. Thomas in the Virgin Islands. A dead chest is a coffin to bury the dead. An island in Sir Francis Drake Channel between St. John and Tortola is called Dead Chest (when viewed from a distance, its silhouette is the shape of a coffin). Probably Dead Chest was a place where fifteen men enjoyed many bottles of rum! It is believed by the islanders of St. Thomas, St. John and Tortola that many treasure chests were buried on the island of Dead Chest.

In the fantasy of every little boy and girl, they have been a daring pirate with a trusty sword sailing the seas in search of adventure and treasure. A favorite costume is the pirate or pirate girl. The entertainment world has provided a frightening but glamorous glimpse of the swashbuckling pirates. The villains of old have been fictionally portrayed as daring, exciting heros.

Does Piracy Still Exist Today?

The Parade magazine in April 1994 reported that as late as 1992, the narrow waterways between Singapore, Malaysia, and Indonesia were home to modern-day pirates who would sail into foreign water, attack a ship and make a quick getaway back into their home waters where they could not be pursued by the foreign navy. In the five years prior to 1993, 523 reported attacks by pirates were documented. These pirates don't play politics; some of these ships were registered American, some Asian countries and some Russian. The treasure today seems to be electronic equipment, valuables and cash, and in some cases the entire ship. Oil tankers are another common victim. A million-dollar yacht was seized by pirates in 1992 off Nice, France.

The Denver Post in May 1993 described the modern methods used in piracy. A high-speed motor launch roared up aft of the victim and grappling hooks caught hold of the freighter's gunwales. The freighter's captain radioed a frantic SOS signal, but passing ships refused to steam to the rescue — they were defenseless against attackers. The Coast Guard ignored his pleas. A dozen or so marauders clambered aboard and rushed barefoot across the deck, slashing the air with razor-edged machetes and yelling for the unarmed captain and crew to surrender. Within only a few minutes, the ship's safe was looted and each crew member was stripped of his personal valuables, cash, boom boxes, wristwatches and rings. The boarders demanded to inspect the holds which contained mining gear bound for Singapore. The raiders hacked the captain to death because they were enraged that the cargo was too bulky to steal.

The predominant area for today's piracy exists in Southeast Asia, a triangle bounded by Hong Kong, the northern Philippine island of Luzon and China's Hainan Island. Since the early 1980s, piracy has been on the upsurge. However, until recently the targets of the seafaring desperadoes were mainly coastal fishing craft or small vessels. Armed with automatic weapons, present-day pirates are increasingly swooping down on lumbering large merchant vessels. Pirates employ high-powered, shallow-draft vessels that are easily able to disappear among the thousands of small islands of the Southeast Asian coastal waters. Meanwhile, daggers and machetes are giving way to military arms, including heavy machine guns, rocket-propelled grenades and AK-47 assault rifles.

International maritime officials report that many pirate attacks are never reported by owners who fear both bad publicity and operating losses.

Today's Pirate

Throughout the United States and the Caribbean, men and women organize as pirate crews. They chose names to reflect their pirate hero or alter ego and identify with the era completely. They hold public events, festivals, parades, re-enactment, medieval fairs, and sail in replicas of early sailing ships. At these events, they dress and speak as 17th and 18th century pirates, cook and eat the food of the period, and stage invasions and battles. They have contests of strength and daring, have singers perform songs of the sea, have storytellers with tales of old, and enjoy a little grog.

The many publications provide opportunity for writers to be published on the subject of piracy and readers to enjoy the current events and controversies.

An entire industry has developed which provides authentic clothing, weapons, flags, books, props, pirate ships, and schools for all who can't resist the lure of the era and the daring of piracy. May it live forever!

Since the dawn of time there have been those who would rather steal from others than earn a living through the sweat of their own brow or the action of their own brain. We call a person a thief, a bandit, a robber, a crook, or a burglar who steals our possessions, but what of the highwaymen of old and the Robin Hood theory of "steal from the rich and give to the poor"? We are accustomed to violence associated with crime because we know if the criminal is determined enough, he does whatever is necessary to get what he wants, murder included.

For the pirates, the idea of stealing for their wealth instead of working for it was not new. On land, theft and robbery and the accompanying violence had been ongoing since before most of the world was civilized. The victims not only lost their wealth, but frequently their life.

It is said there is a little larceny in us all . . . opportunity and greed make the difference!

Since little was written by the pirates themselves, we depend on oral history relayed from generation to generation concerning their activities, and from records of trials and survivors. Some of their stories may have been exaggerated and some may have been too modest, but the influence of piracy on the course of history is dramatic.

The Steam Engine

In the aggressive pursuit of treasure, pirates performed amazing feats of navigation, discovered un-charted harbor sites and channels, and depended on water currents and wind for their water travel. The great age of piracy was hung on the gallows of time by an invention from a man's mind — his facility of reason brought about a ship that did not need sails and did not depend on the wind.

The United States began to experiment with steam power for their naval fleet and advanced their cannonry to include an ex-plosive shell which revolutionized warship construction. Their new ship, invented by Robert Fulton in 1807, used steam for propulsion and the weather didn't affect its movement. A ship powered by the steam engine could go forward, back up, turn and reposition with the turn of a lever which soon made ships with sails obsolete throughout the world. The sailing vessel was king of the open seas until the invention of the steam engine in the 1800s. Between these two poles of man's life on the sea, developed a fascinating history of piracy in days of long ago.

The dire penalties were no deterrent.

GLOSSARY

Variations of nautical terms, the influence of English seamen, different nationalities represented and languages spoken among crew members, and dialects of the Caribbean Islands where they lived, all influenced the vocabulary of pirates. The following includes some of the more interesting common terms and slang used by the salty crewmen.

afoul - entangled or jammed line or anchor; also all manner of woes from a barnacle-covered hull to a captain's wrath

aft - toward the stern or rear of the ship

aloof - to sail as close into the wind as possible; to stand aloof, to keep above or to windward of another vessel

ballast - heavy round stones placed in the bottom of the ship for stability when sailing in rough seas; cargo usually placed on top of ballast stones; barrels or other heavy objects to create balance

beribboned queue - hair style of pirates; hair pulled to the back and tied (pony tail)

bilge - lowest level of a ship's hull where all manner of refuse collected; any stale or worthless remark or idea

binnacle - wooden box located near tiller to hold compass, log, glasses and lamps to read maps

black flag - pirate flag; all black, usually with human skull and crossed bones or swords; many variations

booty - the riches and cargo of a prize; also known as plunder, swag, strike, loot, lucre, treasure

buccaneers - pirates of the Caribbean who learned to cook meat over an open fire until it was dry (called by the natives boucan) Fr.: boucaniers

capstan - an upright circular winch with wooden or iron handles turned by the crew to raise heavy anchors

careen - to scrape, repair and apply pitch and tallow to a ship's hull which had been damaged by heavy seas, teredo worms, or was covered with barnacles which act as a drag and prevent the vessel from slipping easily through the water

cat-o'-nine-tails - whip used to impose punishment of convicted prisoners; nine pieces of knotted rope soaked in tar or vinegar, held together with a short handle; also called cat's tails or simply, the cat

cay - a small island in the Caribbean and the Bahamas

commence all fire power - shooting at the same time towards the enemy ship; some aim at rigging, some at the masts, some rake the deck

copper - a crew member who makes barrels

corsair - pirates, generally in the Mediterranean

corvus - landing platform with large iron spike to strike into the deck of the prize ship to be boarded; a gang way walk; first used by Romans to board Carthaginian ships

crusher - regulating petty officer or ship's policeman on Royal Navy ships

cut and run - to leave in a hurry by cutting the anchor ropes and running before the wind

Davy Jones - the mythical spirit of death who takes charge of drowned pirates and sailors

dead marine - an empty bottle which formerly contained alcohol

dingy - a small ship's boat without sails, using two oars

first among equals - pirate captain who got two shares of a prize

flog - beat with cat-o'-nine-tails as severe punishment

fore - toward the bow or forward on the ship

from the sea - password between two pirate ships as they met at sea

galleon - a fast sailing ship; heavily armed Spanish 16th century cargo vessel

galley - a rowing warship, typically lighter, more slender and lower in the water than a sailing ship; now, a ship's kitchen

gibbet - hanging platform to expose the dead

grappling hook - an iron bar with four or five hooks at one end, tied by a rope at other end, used to snag another ship so as to pull the ship closer to board

grog - alcoholic drink made from rum, water, sugar and lime or lemon juice

gunwale - ribbed railings along the sides of ship about waist high

hanging powder magazine - constructed so as to keep powder casks dry, racks were hung with ropes from ceiling of lower decks to roll with rock of the ship

hemp collar - hangman's rope or noose; hemp halter

hogshead - fifty-five gallon oak cask

hooker - an old and clumsy ship; an affectionate, but disparaging sailor's term for old prostitutes

Jack Dusty - keeper of records for rum disbursement on Royal Navy sailing ships

Jack Nastyface - nickname of cook's assistant on Royal Navy sailing ships

jaunty - the master-at-arms (from the French *gendarme*) who supervised floggings and other disciplinary actions; to swagger about with studied nonchalance

Jolly Roger - a black flag of the pirates with a variation of the skull and crossed bones

junk - worn out roof; or old salted meat that tasted like it

lateen - rig with triangular slanted yard, narrow point of sail set low to the mast

let the cat out of the bag - the ceremony of removing the rawhide cat-o'-nine-tails from its baize carrying bag prior to flogging; later, any untimely, if less serious, revelation

man-of-war - warship heavily armed with cannons; usually three decks

maroon - abandonment on an island or deserted shore; the punishment for an offender who was a traitor or deserter, who abandoned his post in time of battle, or who committed an other significant crime

marooners - escaped African slave pirates in the West Indies who ran away from plantations

match - rope or cord chemically treated to burn at uniform slow rate, used to ignite the cannon charge

merchantmen - a slang name for cargo ships loaded with various trade goods

mortar - short open mouth cannon used to fire fussed round bombs which explode upon contact with the intended target

no quarter - no prisoners taken; no mercy or clemency; represented by red pirate flag

old roger - flag named for the devil in medieval England; displayed cutlasses, sheltons (symbol of death), bleeding hearts; used on various black pirate flags

on the account - code phrase for pirating

pickle - to rub the back with salt and vinegar after flogging

piraqua - canoe hollowed from single log; flat bottom, one sail

poleaxe - large hatchet with sharp point at back of axe head; driving a series of them into a tall ship's side, boarders made an impromptu ladder

pooped - what happened to an unfortunate seaman caught standing on the aft, or poop deck when a giant wave crashed down

port - the left-hand side of a vessel looking toward the bow; any opening in the side of a ship

powder chests - frame of boards joined in form of triangle packed with gunpowder, pebbles, stones, iron shot; set on fire when prize is boarded by pirates to clear the deck

prize - a captured ship with valuable cargo

quarter - mercy shown if the victim surrendered; sparing of life; possibly freedom

quartermaster - a crew member virtually equal to the captain on pirate ships, elected by majority vote

red flag - red for blood, flown on mid-mast to announce to the victim that upon boarding, the pirates were giving no quarter (taking no prisoners); death to all

reef - underwater ridge of coral, rock or sand, close to surface of the sea, near coast and shore lines; unmarked in pirate days

rum rat - a rummy alcoholic on any sailing ship

salmagundi - favorite pirate dish; any marinated cooked meat or seafood mixed with any pickled, raw or cooked vegetables or fruit; usually served cold

salty dog - an insult for a lower class seaman

scuppers - holes cut in ship's side at deck line to drain water in heavy seas

scurvy - a common disease on board ships, later determined to be a dietary deficiency

scuttlebutt - the cask, or butt, that held the ship's daily water ration which had a square hole, or scuttle, at the half-full mark to ensure that only half a butt would be used each day; sailors tarried during water breaks to swap rumors, gossip, or scuttlebutt

shake the cask - dismantling the hoops and tying staves together in a bundle when wooden cask is broken up for later reuse

share out - the act of dividing the loot from a prize according to the Articles of Agreement, usually held on land

shot plug - conical piece of wood driven by carpenters into holes made in ships sides by enemy fire

skedaddle - to sneak away from a working party

slops - clothing sold by the ship's purser, overpriced and usually ill-fitting, thus "sloppy"

slush fund - an illegal fund raised on ships from the sale of grease, rope end and such, used to pay small hard-to-explain expenses

son of a gun - a male child conceived on a gun deck when wives, lovers, and ladies of pleasure were permitted on board while in port

starboard - the right-hand side of a vessel looking toward the bow

stern - rear of the ship; aft

stern chaser - small cannon mounted in stern of ship to fire on pursuer

stranded - to run aground or drift onto a strand or beach

sweet trade - calling to be a pirate in all endeavors, on land or on sea

swivel cannon - small cannon mounted on gun wales, swiveled to enable gunner to shoot in any direction and fire broadside

teredo - a tropical warm-water worm which eats the timbers of a wooden ship causing extensive damage

Tommy Pipes - slang name for boatsman

waft - signal of distress made with a rolled or knotted ensign flying atop the mast of a sailing ship

wild fire - the priming made by wetting gun powder

BIBLIOGRAPHY

Alleyne, Warren: <u>Caribbean Pirates</u>, The Macmillan Press Ltd., Hong Kong, 1986.

American Heritage: <u>Pirates of the Spanish Main</u>, Narrative by Hamilton Cochran, American Heritage Publishing Co., New York, 1961.

Botting, Douglas: <u>The Pirates</u>, (The Seafarers Series), Time-Life Books, Alexandria, VA, 1978.

Cabal, Juan: <u>Piracy & Pirates, A History</u>, Jarrolds Publishers Ltd., London, 1957.

Carse, Robert: <u>The Age of Piracy</u>, Grosset & Dunlap, New York, 1957.

Clarke, Nell Ray: "The Haunts of the Caribbean Corsairs," <u>National Geographic</u>, Vol. 16 No. 2, February 1922.

Cordingly, David and John Falconer: <u>Pirates: Fact & Fiction</u>, Abbeville Publishing Group, New York, 1992.

Defoe, Daniel: <u>A General History of the Pyrates</u>, edited by Manuel Schonhorn, University of South Carolina Press, Columbia, SC, 1972. (Originally published in 1724.)

de la Varende, Jean: <u>Cherish the Sea</u>, The Viking Press, New York, 1956.

Esquemeling, Alexander Olivier (John): <u>The Buccaneers of America</u>, (originally published in Dutch in 1684), The Rio Grande Press, Inc., Glorieta, NM, 1992.

Feder, Joshua B.: <u>Pirates</u>, Mallard Press, New York, 1992.

Fitzgibbon, Russell H., and Flaud C. Wooton: <u>Latin America, Past and Present</u>, D. C. Heath & Co., New York, 1946.

Hendrickson, Robert: <u>Ocean Almanac</u>, Doubleday, New York, 1984.

<u>Islands, An International Magazine</u>, Vol. 14 No 4, Islands Publishing Co., Santa Barbara, CA, July/August 1994.

Lampe, Christine Markel and Michael Lampe: <u>No Quarter Given</u>, Vol. I-V, The Lampes, Riverside, CA , 1994-98.

Lewisohn, Florence: <u>Tales of Tortola and the British Virgin Islands</u>, Published by the author, 1966.

Mathewson, R. Duncan, III: <u>Treasure of the Atocha</u>, Pisces Books, New York, 1986.

Milanich, Jerald T. and Susan Milbrath: <u>First Encounters: Spanish Explorations in the Caribbean and the United States, 1492-1750</u>, University of Florida Press, Gainesville, FL, 1989.

Mitchell, Carleton: <u>Isles of the Caribees</u>, The National Geographic Society, Washington, DC, 1966.

Oakley, Amy: <u>Behold the West Indies</u>, D. Appleton-Century Co., NY, 1943.

Pack, James A.: <u>Nelson's Blood, the Story of Naval Rum</u>, Kenneth Mason Publisher, Hampshire, England, 1982.

Parry, J. H. and Phillip Sherlock: <u>A Short History of the West Indies</u>, St. Martin's Press, New York, 1956

Scofield, John: "Christopher Columbus and the New World He Found," <u>National Geographic</u>, Vol. 148 No. 5, November 1975.

Sherry, Frank: <u>Raiders and Rebels, The Golden Age of Piracy</u>, William Morrow & Company, New York, 1986.

<u>The International Journal of Nautical Archaeology</u>, Nautical Archaeology Society, Vol. 17 No. 1, Academic Press Ltd., London, February 1988.

<u>The Pirates Own Book: Authentic Narratives of the Most Celebrated Sea Robbers</u>, Marine Research Society (originally published 1924), Dover Publications, Inc., New York, 1993.

Ward, Ralph T.: <u>Pirates in History</u>, York Press, Baltimore, MD, 1974.

Whipple, A. B. C.: <u>Fighting Sail</u> (The Seafarers Series), Time-Life Books, Alexandria, VA, 1978.

Winston, Alexander: <u>No Man Knows My Grave</u>, Houghton Mifflin Company, Boston, MA, 1969.

Woodbury, George: <u>The Great Days of Piracy in the West Indies</u>, W. W. Norton & Co., New York, 1951

Our special thanks to the artists and illustrators who generously provided their art and photography for *Piracy — Days of Long Ago*. We are grateful!

Rick Reeves, historical print artist, Tampa, Florida
Front Cover - "Blackbeard"
Inside front cover - "Searching for New
                Opportunities"
Page 42 - "Bartholomew Roberts"
Page 43 - "Settled Accounts"
Page 46 - "A Difference of Opinion"
Page 47 - "Dead Men Tell No Tales"

Richard Becker, Redwood City, California
Page 35 - "The Privateer"
Page 52 - "Sad Dog"
Page 56 - "The Gun Captain"
Page 70 - "Not Enough for Two"
Pages 33, 52, 53, 55, 57, 58, 64, 66 - illustrations
                from Bloodthirsty Pirate Tales
Back cover - "My Treasure"

Gene Packwood, Dona Vista, Florida
Page 4 - "The New World"
Page 24 - "The Boucaniers"
Page 34 - "A Band of Cutthroats"
Page 38 - "Ready to Attack"
Page 39 - "A Short Life and a Merry One!"
Page 50 - "Life Aboard Ship"
Page 71 - "Infamous Pirate"

Mel Fisher, Treasure Salvors, Inc., Key West, Florida
Inside back cover - photographs by Pat Clyne and Don Kincaid of artifacts recovered by the Mel Fisher Expeditions.

*   *   *   *   *   *   *

The Florida Department of Education, through the Florida Instructional Materials Center for the Visually Impaired in Tampa, received permission from the author to prepare *Piracy – Days of Long Ago* in Braille and recorded versions for the visually impaired students in Florida's schools. Ken Mulder was honored by their request and is proud to have this publication chosen to be included in their statewide distribution. Call 1-800-282-9193 (in Florida) for information.

To order additional copies of *Piracy – Days of Long Ago* and other publications by Ken Mulder:

Piracy — Days of Long Ago:	$14.95
Seminoles — Days of Long Ago:	5.95
Tampa Bay — Days of Long Ago:	4.95

Shipping & handling (1 book or all 3):   3.00
Florida residents include Florida State Sales Tax

Make check payable to: Ken Mulder
and mail to: **Mulder Enterprises**
                P.O. Box 320935
                Tampa, FL 33679

Write or call (813/837-6325) for quantity pricing.

\#   \#   \#   \#   \#   \#   \#

To order prints by Rick Reeves:

Dead Men Tell No Tales
limited edition print, 18" x 23" $85.00 ea
A Difference of Opinion
limited edition print, 24" x 18"   65.00 ea
Blackbeard, Settled Accounts, Bartholomew Roberts, Searching for New Opportunities
open edition prints, 11" x 14"   20.00 ea
Package of four open edition prints   65.00/set

Include $10.00 shipping and handling per item (or package of four). Florida residents include Florida State Sales Tax.

Make check payable to: Collector Historical Prints, Inc.
Mail to: **P.O. Box 18661**
            Tampa, FL 33679
Telephone (813) 877-9334

\#   \#   \#   \#   \#   \#   \#

Illustrations by Richard Becker are from **"Bloodthirsty Pirate Tales"**. Issues available:
        Issue 1 - $6.00
        Issue 2 - $3.00
        Issues 3, 4, 5 and 6 - $2.50 each
        Issue 7 - $2.95
Shipping & handling, add $2.00. California residents include 8.25% tax.

Make check payable to: Richard Becker
Mail to: **Black Swan Press**
            204 Winslow Street
            Redwood City, CA 94063-1347

Pirating from one author is *plagiarism*; pirating from many authors is *research*. This is a book of *research*. KWM

Royal seal of
Philip IV

Roman numeral
and dot indicating
21¼ karats purity

Assayer's "bite"

Mysterious
"En Rada" stamp

Figure 1. Among the treasures of the *Atocha* was this one-pound, five-ounce gold bar. Like all other precious metals leaving the New World, gold bars were meticulously marked with stamps and seals noting the purity of the bars, the mint where they were cast, and whether the King's tax had been paid. Gold bars shipped legally show an assayer's "bite", a gouge where a small piece of the bar has been taken to test its purity. This bar bears the cryptic legend "En Rada," another of the mysteries of the *Atocha*.

Figure 2. Solid gold surrounds over 400 diamonds represented by the two brooches and earring set. All pieces were recovered near Sebastian, Florida, from the wreck sites of the 1715 Spanish Plate Fleet.

Figure 3. This exquisite ring of solid gold with a single emerald (detailed above) and the cross *(figure 5)* were found inside a silver jewelry case recovered from the *Atocha*. Rings were associated with love and marriage. The devout wore rings bearing emblems of faith, and Popes and bishops wore rings as a sign of their authority and their wealth.

Figure 4. Three artifacts of pure gold representing the fine and intricate work of the Spanish goldsmiths. A Rosary, manicure set, and filigree picture frame recovered from the wreck sites of the 1715 Spanish Plate Fleet on Florida's east coast.

Figure 5. The most popular religious item was the cross. It was the main symbol of the Christian faith and considered a powerful talisman that would bring good fortune to the faithful. The 65-karat emerald in the cross came from the mine in the Muzo district of Colombia. The reverse side of this magnificent cross *(left)* is engraved with the image of a saint and the Madonna holding the Christ child.

Background. A closeup of a gold "money chain" from the *Margarita*. Links could be bent off and used in business transactions. Each link is individually handmade and weighs the same, thought to relate to the gold escudo coins of the 17th century.

All artifacts on inside cover from the Mel Fisher collection, Key West, FL.